# THE ULTIMATE SELF-LOVE HANDBOOK FOR TEEN GIRLS

CRUSH PEER PRESSURE, DEFEAT SOCIAL MEDIA
STEREOTYPES, EMBRACE YOUR BEAUTY, AND EXCEL
IN SCHOOL

## MAUREEN GIANNOTTI

# CONTENTS

# INTRODUCTION

Close your eyes for a moment and visualize the extraordinary Malala Yousafzai. She stands before you, a shining star of courage and determination. Her story is an epic of unwavering commitment, a tale of remarkable strength that transcends the ordinary.

Malala didn't just face adversity; she stared it down, unflinching, even in the face of a gun barrel pointed at her. While most of us might wither in such circumstances, Malala emerged even more radiant and empowered from the shadows. Her story is not a fleeting spark in the night but a blazing comet that streaks across the sky, illuminating the path for us all.

Why is Malala's story especially vital for young girls like you? It's because she shattered the constraints of her society to champion girls' rights to receive an education. She dared to dream bigger and bolder in a world where such dreams were often suppressed. Her life is an inspiration, a testament to the idea that no obstacle is insurmountable, no height unattainable, and no dream too audacious.

Her journey isn't just an ode to her indomitable spirit; it's a lesson for every young girl who faces challenges, doubts, or obstacles. Malala's story says you can make a difference regardless of your circumstances or origin. Her tale reminds us that your voice, your dreams, your aspirations—they all matter. They matter immensely.

Now, let's delve into some numbers, but don't worry, I promise it won't be the usual mind-numbing kind. These statistics are like a magnifying glass, offering a sharp focus on a daunting reality that we're here to confront head-on.

Imagine this: Over 70% of girls aged 15–17, girls just like you, often find themselves avoiding everyday activities when they're feeling disheartened about their looks (*11 Facts About Teens and Self-Esteem*, 2015). Whether it's the fear of judgment, comparison, or societal expectations, the weight of self-doubt can suffocate. It's like a shadow that looms over the sunniest days, hindering you from embracing life's beauty.

But the story doesn't end there; it gets even more astonishing and sobering. A whopping 75% of girls with low self-esteem resort to negative behaviors as their coping mechanism (*11 Facts About Teens and Self-Esteem*, 2015). These aren't mere numbers; they represent the daily struggles that many young women face. From self-harm, cutting through the pain, to the darkness of bullying, from the dangers of smoking to the torment of disordered eating, these struggles are the silent battles fought behind closed doors.

The truly remarkable contrast is the 25% of girls with high self-esteem who've found a different path. They've discovered the strength within to choose healthier, more empowering ways to navigate the complexities of teenage life.

But let's make one clear: These statistics aren't just numbers; they're reflections of the lives, challenges, and triumphs of girls like you. Your struggles and self-doubt are not isolated or unique; they're part of a shared experience.

After all, you might have felt the searing pang of public humiliation, an experience that lingers long after the spotlight has moved on. Perhaps it was that discouraging failing grade that cast doubt on your abilities, a scar that remains hidden beneath the surface. Or maybe the Instagram post garnered not a single like, making you question your place in the world of digital approval. Remember, a book's title is just the beginning; it's the fuel for the fire smoldering within you, those concealed anxieties and silent cries longing for release. It's the realization that you deserve more, and it's the first step toward your transformation.

Imagine effortlessly conquering your homework, armed with newfound study techniques that banish late-night cramming and headaches. It's like holding the key to academic success in your hand. Visualize yourself striding into a room full of judgmental eyes, leaving a trail of admiration and respect in your wake. You'll radiate self-assuredness, your secret weapon that commands attention. This time, you're the star, and the storyline revolves around your growth, empowerment, and unwavering love for yourself.

Consider the enchanting journey of Billie Eilish, a true force of nature in the music industry. Billie's rise to stardom, driven by her unshakable self-belief, is another sparkling gem that adorns our book's value proposition. It's a reminder that even the most extraordinary achievements begin with a belief in one's potential.

These stories remind you that your dreams can take flight and your voice can resonate worldwide. You're on the cusp of something extraordinary; this book is your guiding star.

You won't be alone on this incredible journey. You're probably wondering who I am and why you should trust me with your teenage woes. Let me be frank with you, just like I'd be with my teenage self. I've been in your shoes. Yes, you heard that right. I've faced the teenage storm, the doubts, and the insecurities. And with help, I got through the other side in one piece. However, I felt like I fumbled through, just like you might be feeling now.

Well, I'm more than just an author. I'm a devoted wife, a mother, a Shamanic Practitioner, and an Animal Reiki Practitioner/Teacher. My connection to the spiritual realm and my work with teens have given me a front-row seat to the struggles and triumphs of parenting a teen daughter. I'm not just here to offer advice; I want to be your guiding light, ally, and confidante.

Now, let's gaze into the future and unveil the dazzling result awaiting you after you've devoured the wisdom within these pages. Picture this: a life glowing with self-love, a radiant confidence that rivals the sun's golden rays. Your courage, once wavering, will become as unshakeable as a skyscraper, enabling you to stand tall in the face of challenges that used to feel insurmountable. And those grades, which once caused you to furrow your brow, will transform your refrigerator door into a gallery of excellence adorned with the symbols of your academic triumphs.

Before you turned the pages of this book, life may have felt like trying to solve a Rubik's Cube blindfolded, each twist and turn leading you further into a maze of confusion. But now, every challenge aligns, making what once seemed impossible appear as child's play.

By now, you're likely feeling it in your bones—this is the right book for you. It's not just another title on the shelf; it's your personal blueprint, your insider's guide to the teen years you've been secretly craving but never knew existed. It's your roadmap to self-discovery, empowerment, and a future brimming with possibilities. Welcome to a transformative journey that will change your life.

1

---

# SELF-LOVE IS YOUR NEW SUPERPOWER!

Ariana Grande had it right when she sang, "I've learned from the pain, turned out amazing." We've all been through some stuff, but here's the secret: The magic ingredient to turning out amazing is self-love!

This is your backstage pass to understanding what self-love is all about, and guess what? It's not just about spa days and bubble baths (although those are fabulous, too). Self-love is about embracing who you are, warts and all, and celebrating the fabulous uniqueness that is you.

Now, I know what you might think: "Isn't self-love just a fancy way of saying 'selfish'?" Well, buckle up because we're about to dismantle that myth and put the "self" back in "selfless." You'll discover that self-love isn't selfish; it's a fundamental human right and your superpower for navigating the world with confidence and kindness.

Soon, you'll have a rock-solid understanding of self-love and how to nurture it. We're going to equip you with a self-love inventory that's like your very own superhero gear, helping you gauge where you stand on your self-love journey.

## WHY IS SELF-LOVE YOUR NEW SUPERPOWER?

As we unlock your superpower of self-love, let's begin by dismantling a stubborn myth: the notion that self-love is an egotistical indulgence. In a world where humility is celebrated, it's easy to misunderstand self-love as vanity or self-centered-ness. But the truth couldn't be farther from that misconception.

Self-love isn't about putting yourself above others or thinking you're the center of the universe. It's about acknowledging your worth, just as you recognize the worth of others. Think of it as filling your cup so you have abundant love, kindness, and positivity to share with those around you.

In this era of instant gratification, it's easy to fall into the trap of equating online approval with self-worth. The more thumbs-ups, hearts, and comments you receive, the more you may feel valued and validated. But what happens when those digital gestures of approval stop rolling in? It's like building a house on shaky ground. The foundation of your self-worth becomes contingent on the unpredictable whims of your virtual audience.

To truly flourish in the digital age and beyond, we need to understand the fundamental difference between online approval and authentic self-worth.

As we move forward in this journey, always remember this: Self-love is the real deal, your new superpower, and it's far from selfish. It's the foundation for self-confidence, resilience, and authentic happiness. Let's continue to explore the art of self-love and discover how it can serve as your emotional armor in the digital age and every facet of your life.

## THE REAL TALK: WHY YOU'RE STRUGGLING WITH LOVING YOURSELF

Have you ever wondered why embracing self-love isn't as straightforward as it might seem? The journey to self-love is often hindered by subtle culprits that lurk in the shadows, undermining our efforts. These culprits, influenced mainly by societal norms, familial expectations, and our own experiences, have stealthily molded our self-perception. You see, we might find it challenging to prioritize self-love because, deep down, we've absorbed the notion that focusing on ourselves can be seen as "selfish." There's this underlying fear that if we dedicate too much time to self-care and self-compassion, we will somehow be left unable to provide the support, love, and care that we believe we owe to others.

This hesitation to put ourselves first stems from a long-ingrained mindset that insists that always putting others before ourselves is the path of virtue. However, the truth is quite the opposite. By embracing self-love and caring for ourselves first, we're not draining our capacity to care for others; we're filling our reservoirs. It's like the oxygen mask on an airplane—you secure your mask first so that you're in the best position to help those around you. Thus, acknowledging and confronting these societal norms, familial expectations, and personal experiences is an essential step in unlocking the path to genuine self-love.

### The Shackles of Societal Norms

Societal norms shape our perception of what is considered "normal" or "desirable." Magazines, TV shows, and social media relentlessly bombard us with images of the "ideal" body, the "perfect" lifestyle, and the "happiest" relationships. It's no surprise that many of us end up feeling like we don't measure up.

### The Weight of Familial Expectations

Family plays a significant role in shaping our self-esteem. Well-meaning parents and relatives often have specific hopes and dreams for us. Whether it's academic success, a particular career, or even a certain lifestyle, these expectations can feel like a heavy burden.

### Personal Experiences: The Silent Architects of Self-Perception

Personal experiences, both positive and negative, leave indelible imprints on our self-perception. Traumatic events like bullying, a painful breakup, or the loss of a loved one can deeply affect how we see ourselves.

## SIGNS OF THE LACK OF SELF-LOVE

Understanding the signs that may indicate a lack of self-love in your own life is essential for growth. Recognizing these signs can be the first step toward healing and nurturing self-love. Some of these signs include:

- **Negative self-talk and self-criticism**: Constantly berating yourself and focusing on your flaws.
- **Seeking constant validation from others:** Relying on external affirmation for your self-worth.
- **Perfectionism:** Setting impossibly high standards for yourself.
- **Comparing yourself to others:** Measuring your worth against the successes of others.
- **Fear of failure:** A paralyzing fear of making mistakes or not meeting expectations.
- **Difficulty setting boundaries:** Struggling to say no and overextending yourself.
- **Avoidance of self-care:** Neglecting your physical and emotional needs.
- **Feeling unworthy of love and happiness:** Believing that you don't deserve love, joy, or success.

If any of these signs resonate with you, it's okay. Acknowledging them is the first step on your journey to self-love. You're not alone, and there's a path toward transformation. Together, we will unravel the mysteries of these culprits, confront them head-on, and pave the way for a healthier, more loving relationship with ourselves. It's a journey of self-discovery and growth, and it starts with understanding and compassion for our own unique story.

## THE COMPONENTS OF AUTHENTIC SELF-LOVE

It's time to unravel the amazing components that make up self-love: self-acceptance, self-compassion, and self-respect. Think of these as your trusty sidekicks, each with their own unique superpowers, coming together to create an unstoppable force against negativity. So, put on your capes, and let's dive into the world of self-love superheroes!

As Borenstein (2020, para. 2) eloquently puts it, self-love is "a state of appreciation for oneself that grows from actions that support our physical, psychological, and spiritual growth." It's the art of cherishing your own well-being and happiness, pledging to care for your needs without compromising your own happiness to appease others. Self-love is about refusing to accept anything less than what you truly deserve.

Furthermore, as Borenstein (2020, para. 6) beautifully articulates, self-love entails embracing your present self, complete with all your imperfections, and prioritizing your physical, emotional, and mental well-being above all else.

But here's the exciting revelation from Cooks-Campbell (2022, para. 3): Self-love is not an innate trait but a skill that you can develop, much like nurturing self-confidence or self-trust. This skill is a vitally important one on your journey of self-discovery.

Think of embarking on the path of self-love as you would approach the start of a new, exciting relationship, as Cooks-Campbell (2022) suggests. Just like when you make a new friend, date someone special, or care for a new houseplant, there's a learning curve. It's an opportunity to ask questions, experiment, learn what works and what doesn't, and remain curious and engaged as you nurture this beautiful connection with yourself.

Martin (2019) encapsulates self-love as a comprehensive practice of embracing yourself entirely, treating yourself with kindness and respect, and fostering your personal growth and well-being. Self-love extends to how you treat yourself and the thoughts and emotions you harbor about your own self-worth, as Martin (2019) underscores. In essence, it involves being your own best friend, offering yourself love, and embracing a mindset filled with warmth and self-concern.

So, as we set off on this exhilarating adventure into the world of self-love superheroes, remember that these superpowers—self-acceptance, self-compassion, and self-respect—unite to empower you to face life's challenges with inner strength, unwavering compassion, and the belief that you truly deserve all the love and happiness the world has to offer.

### *Self-Acceptance: Embrace Your Unique Superpowers*

Imagine self-acceptance as your personal cheerleader, always there to support you. It's all about embracing your true self, quirks and all. Instead of trying to fit into someone else's mold, it's about celebrating your unique qualities.

Self-acceptance is about welcoming yourself as you are without any judgments (Ackerman, 2018a). When you fully accept yourself, you embrace your strengths, weaknesses, and all the things that make you, well, you.

### *Self-Compassion: Be Your Own Superhero Sidekick*

Simply put, the journey to self-love involves getting to know and appreciate the wonderful person you are deep inside. At the same time, nurturing self-compassion means treating yourself with kindness and understanding, just as you would with your dearest friend. This process of self-discovery and self-awareness is a beautiful and essential part of learning to embrace and love yourself.

Now, think of self-compassion as your trusty superhero sidekick. It's like a warm and comforting hug when you need it most. It's all about treating yourself with kindness, just as you would treat a superhero buddy. It's the power of self-love that helps you bounce back from challenging situations with a heart full of understanding.

Self-compassion can be broken down into three simple parts:

- self-kindness
- understanding that everyone makes mistakes
- staying in the present moment with loads of self-compassion

It's like having a superhero cape wrapped around you, but it's made of kindness and self-love. Self-compassion can only be built if we begin to "forgive ourselves for our mistakes and turn them into learning opportunities" (Cooks-Campbell, 2022, para. 25).

### Self-Respect: Claim Your Superhero Throne

Say hello to self-respect, your superhero leader on the path to self-love and self-care. Imagine it as your majestic crown, which boldly proclaims, "I am awesome!" Self-respect is your unwavering recognition of your worth, your boundless reservoir of strength, and your guide in ensuring that the world treats you with the reverence you deserve.

As Cooks-Campbell (2022) aptly points out, learning to take care of yourself involves building habits that support your overall well-being. It's like donning a superhero cape and taking center stage in your life's story. This means not only recognizing your incredible worth but also taking bold actions to uphold it. Think of it as setting superhero-style boundaries— a clear and invincible shield against any negativity or disrespect that may come your way. It's about standing firm in your beliefs, unapologetically saying "no" to anything that doesn't align with your self-love values, and ensuring that the world treats you with the honor a superhero deserves. Don't forget to create a self-care plan, just like a superhero strategizing their next mission. This plan will serve as your secret weapon, ensuring you're consistently recharged and ready to face any challenge that comes your way.

### *The Unbreakable Shield of Self-Love*

Now, picture these three superhero traits coming together like an incredible shield. Self-acceptance forms a sturdy base, allowing you to be your true superhero self. Self-compassion is the warm and comforting layer that helps you bounce back from life's challenges with kindness. Self-respect acts as the protective outer shell, shielding you from negativity and nonsense.

When you bring self-acceptance, self-compassion, and self-respect together, you create an unbreakable superhero shield. This shield empowers you to conquer self-doubt, laugh off criticism, and stand strong against societal pressures, all while staying true to the incredible superhero you are.

## HOW SELF-LOVE CHANGES EVERYTHING

Self-love is not just a personal secret; it's the magical ingredient that can transform every part of your life. Think of it as your compass, your North Star guiding you through the chaotic maze of adolescence with style and grace.

Self-love isn't just about looking in the mirror and thinking, "I look good today." It's a superpower that seeps into every crevice of your world. Let's take an adventure and explore how self-love works its magic on your relationships, academics, and every corner of your life.

### *The Impact on Relationships*

Imagine you have a friend who radiates self-love. They're confident, know their worth, and aren't afraid to set boundaries. How does that affect your friendship? It's like a ripple effect. Your friend's self-love sets the bar for a healthy and respectful relationship. They inspire you to embrace your self-worth and demand respect from your friends.

Now, flip the scenario: You meet someone who doesn't love themselves. They're clingy, constantly seek validation, and struggle with jealousy. It's like a storm cloud that follows them, creating turbulence in their relationships. Self-love can be the sunshine that disperses those clouds, helping people build healthier connections based on trust and mutual respect.

Adolescence can feel like a perplexing maze, full of unexpected turns and challenging puzzles. It's a time of change, growth, and self-discovery. Self-love is like the magical map that guides you through these twists and turns with grace.

The message is clear: Self-love isn't just a solitary endeavor; it's a transformational force. It helps you build strong and respectful relationships, excel academically, and navigate the twists and turns of adolescence with a sense of purpose and confidence. As we continue our journey, we will delve into practical tools and strategies to strengthen your self-love superpower, empowering you to embrace all the incredible opportunities that adolescence offers.

ACTIVITY: YOUR SELF-LOVE CHECK-IN—A
QUICK QUIZ

Discover where you stand on the self-love scale by answering
the following questions. Be honest with yourself, and choose
the option that best describes your feelings or behaviors in each
situation.

1. How do you react to compliments?

    A. I accept them graciously and believe I deserve them.
    B. I feel awkward but thank the person for the
    compliment.
    C. I brush them off or think they must be insincere.

2. When you make a mistake or fail at something, how do you
typically react?

    A. I acknowledge the mistake, learn from it, and move on
    with self-compassion.
    B. I feel disappointed but understand that everyone
    makes mistakes.
    C. I'm very hard on myself and believe I'm a failure.

3. How do you handle criticism or negative feedback?

    A. I listen, reflect, and consider if there's something I can
    learn from it.
    B. I take it in stride, knowing that not everyone will
    always agree with me.

C. I get defensive, feel hurt, and believe it's a personal attack.

4. In your friendships and relationships, do you feel you can set boundaries?

A. Yes, I'm comfortable setting boundaries and communicating them clearly.
B. I can, but sometimes I feel guilty about it.
C. No, I often let people cross my boundaries because I don't want to upset them.

5. When you look in the mirror, what are your thoughts?

A. I see a reflection of someone who is unique and worthy of love and respect.
B. I have mixed feelings but try to focus on my positive qualities.
C. I'm often critical of myself and focus on flaws or imperfections.

6. How do you feel about your accomplishments and achievements?

A. I celebrate them as signs of my hard work and capabilities.
B. I'm proud of my achievements but sometimes doubt their significance.
C. I downplay my accomplishments and feel like I got lucky.

7. How often do you prioritize self-care and relaxation time?

A. Regularly, I understand the importance of self-care and make time for it.

B. Occasionally, but I sometimes feel guilty for taking time for myself.

C. Rarely, I feel like I should always be productive and put others first.

**Scoring Key**

- For every "A" response, give yourself 3 points.
- For every "B" response, give yourself 2 points.
- For every "C" response, give yourself 1 point.

**Interpreting Your Score**

- **18–21 points:** You're rocking the self-love game! You have a strong foundation of self-love, and it's reflected in how you handle various life situations. Keep nurturing and celebrating yourself.
- **12–17 points:** You're on the right path, but there's room for growth. While you have moments of self-love, there are areas where you can be kinder to yourself. Consider focusing on self-compassion and setting healthier boundaries.
- **7—11 points:** Self-love may be an area where you need more attention. Remember, self-love is a journey, and you can start by practicing self-compassion and

working on setting boundaries. Your well-being is worth it!

Use this quiz as a starting point to gauge your self-love and discover areas where you can enhance it. Remember, self-love is an ongoing practice, and every step you take brings you closer to a stronger, more confident, and happier you.

## AFFIRMATION SECTION: YOUR PERSONAL MANTRAS FOR SELF-LOVE

Affirmations are like little magic spells you cast on yourself. They're positive statements that, when repeated regularly, can rewire your thought patterns and boost your self-love. The more you immerse yourself in these uplifting words, the more your brain believes them, creating a shift in your self-perception.

### Your Daily Dose of Affirmations

- "I am enough."
- "I am deserving of love and happiness."
- "I embrace my imperfections."
- "I am in charge of my thoughts and emotions."
- "I attract positive people and experiences into my life."
- "I forgive myself for my mistakes."
- "I set healthy boundaries to protect my well-being."
- "I am resilient and can overcome any challenge."
- "I am in control of my own happiness."
- "I love and accept myself unconditionally."

## *Making Affirmations a Daily Ritual*

The key to making these affirmations work their magic is repetition. Here's how to make it a part of your daily routine:

1. Choose a quiet moment in your day, like when you wake up or before bed.
2. Say the affirmations out loud, looking at yourself in the mirror if possible.
3. Feel the words as you say them. Believe in their truth.
4. Repeat them with sincerity, even if it feels awkward at first.

Over time, these affirmations will weave into the fabric of your being, creating a mental landscape of self-love and positivity. Remember, just like taking daily vitamins, affirmations are a daily dose of self-love and self-belief. They're your soul's way of saying, "I love you" to yourself.

2

---

# STAND YOUR GROUND AGAINST
# PEER PRESSURE

A s Taylor Swift once beautifully sang, "You are not the opinion of someone who doesn't know you." This resonates deeply, especially when tackling the sometimes-overwhelming world of peer pressure.

Imagine this: You're standing at a crossroads in life, and it feels like everyone has an opinion about how you should go. Your friends, schoolmates, and the constant buzz of social media are all pulling at your decision-making. It's like a game of tug-of-war between staying true to who you are and giving in to the pressures that surround you.

But remember, your uniqueness isn't defined by what others think. You're a masterpiece woven from your dreams, quirks, and values.

Unlike adults, it can be challenging for kids and teens to express their feelings. "Students are experiencing stress at growing rates, with a 2014 American Psychological Association study finding teens in the U.S. are even more stressed than adults" (Staff Writers, 2019, para. 2).

Peer pressure is something that approximately 90% of teenagers have experienced. It's commonly seen as any outside influence that might affect your physical or mental well-being (Centerstone, 2022). You need to understand that peer pressure isn't always a bad thing. It can be positive, like when your friends encourage you to take part in a play, push you to excel in your studies, or nudge you to try new foods (Centerstone, 2022). But it can also take a negative turn, restricting your independence or leading to emotional and physical consequences.

## WHAT PEER PRESSURE REALLY LOOKS LIKE

So, you might think you've got peer pressure all figured out, right? It's about being dared to do something or someone explicitly telling you what to do. Well, think again! Peer pressure is a shapeshifter, and it extends far beyond the obvious. It's like an invisible force that often sneaks into our lives in ways we might not even notice.

You might think it's all about someone daring you to do stuff or being directly told what to do, but it's actually a lot sneakier than that. It's like this invisible force that can creep into our lives in ways we might not even notice.

Think about it: You're at a crossroads, and it feels like everyone's got an opinion on which path you should take. Your friends, your classmates, and even the folks you follow on social media are all trying to influence your choices. It's like a tugging match between staying true to yourself and giving in to the pressures around you.

But you know what? Peer pressure isn't always in-your-face obvious. As Muffett (2021) points out, it can be as subtle as just seeing others do something that seems risky or not so smart. You see them having a blast, and suddenly, you feel the pull to join in. Why does this happen? Well, it's got a lot to do with how our teenage brains work.

And it's not just about being dared to do wild things; peer pressure can also affect decisions and habits, especially when it comes to stuff like alcohol and drugs. AspenRidge Recovery (2021) brings up how it's a real influencer here, and it's a topic that's not exactly a walk in the park to understand.

Have you ever heard of the social learning theory in psychology? This theory suggests that we learn and pick up new behaviors by watching and imitating others. It's like a big blending pot of influences, from parents and teachers to friends and even celebrities. AspenRidge Recovery (2021) reminds us how this theory plays a role in peer pressure—it's all part of our interconnected world.

So, here's the deal, my fabulous friends: Peer pressure is a whole lot more complex than it seems. It's not just about someone daring you. It's about those invisible nudges and pulls you might not even be aware of. But guess what? You've got the power to make your own choices, stay true to yourself, and not let peer pressure rule the game.

## PEER PRESSURE MISCONCEPTIONS

Peer pressure, often misconstrued, transcends the stereotypical image of rebellious teenagers daring each other to engage in risky endeavors. While this is one facet of the phenomenon, peer pressure extends deeper and broader than commonly perceived.

Daring someone to partake in an action represents merely the tip of the iceberg. Peer pressure can subtly manifest when friends nonchalantly mention their lifestyle choices, leading you to question your own. It can insidiously infiltrate seemingly innocuous conversations or embed itself within the choices and behaviors of those in your immediate circle.

Peer pressure isn't confined to adolescence; it's a constant companion throughout one's life, influencing individuals of all ages. For teenagers, it may revolve around seeking acceptance within a specific peer group. However, for adults, it takes on diverse forms, such as workplace dynamics, societal expectations, or pressure from friends to conform to certain norms.

It's not solely friends who exert peer pressure; family, media, and society also play significant roles. Parents might pressure their children to emulate their career paths or adhere to cultural norms. The media wields the power to set trends and sway personal choices, while society can exert pressure to conform to specific behaviors and beliefs.

Peer pressure ranges from a gentle nudge to a hurricane's force, not always conspicuous; at times, it whispers, encouraging you to follow the crowd.

## THE SNEAKY WAYS PEER PRESSURE SHOWS UP

Peer pressure, a shapeshifter that adapts to various guises, can emerge in distinct forms, spanning the spectrum from overt to covert, resembling a chameleon that blends into different social contexts.

The most overt and easily identifiable form is spoken peer pressure, wherein someone explicitly urges, encourages, or challenges you to take specific actions. This might manifest when a friend says, "Come on, just try it, it's fun!" or "Don't be a chicken; take the risk!" Spoken peer pressure confronts you head-on, making its presence conspicuous.

In contrast, unspoken peer pressure operates more subtly. While no one verbally attempts to influence your choices, an unspoken group norm silently dictates certain behaviors. This pressure is akin to a silent influence in the room, where no one explicitly instructs you, yet you keenly feel the weight of unspoken expectations. It could be the implicit rule that prescribes a particular dress code for a party or the subtle push to attain top grades because it is the prevailing standard. Unspoken pressure can be elusive since it lurks in the ambiance and unspoken anticipations. Picture yourself at a party where everyone adheres to a specific style without anyone dictating it, yet you sense the unspoken expectation compelling you to conform.

Direct peer pressure targets you personally, with someone actively urging you to conform to their desires. It's analogous to a friend insisting you attend a party against your will or someone persistently encouraging you to skip class. This form is personal and pointed, leaving no ambiguity about their intentions.

On the other hand, indirect peer pressure is less explicit but equally influential, stemming from your observations of others' actions and choices. For example, witnessing your friends posting pictures of themselves partying on social media might instill in you a desire to do the same. Indirect peer pressure can be subtle and insidious, making you feel the decisions are your own, even though external factors heavily influence them.

Negative peer pressure steers you toward harmful or risky behaviors, coaxing you into engaging in activities that can have adverse consequences, such as smoking, drinking, or skipping school. It frequently leads you down a dangerous path that undermines your well-being. Consider a group of friends who press you to try smoking a cigarette, even if you've consistently been opposed to it. They epitomize negative peer pressure by enticing you toward a dangerous choice.

In contrast, positive peer pressure encourages constructive decisions. It's akin to friends motivating you to excel in your studies, participate in sports, or engage in volunteer work. This form of peer pressure fosters your personal growth and well-being. An instance of positive peer pressure is when your friends invite you to partake in a community service project, their encouragement propelling you toward a positive choice and inspiring you to contribute to your community.

## ANATOMY OF A FRENEMY: NOT ALL FRIENDS ARE ALLIES

Friendship is a delightful journey filled with shared laughter, memorable adventures, and unwavering support. But not all companions on this journey are true friends. Sometimes, you may encounter individuals who walk the fine line between friendship and something entirely different—frenemies.

A frenemy, at its core, is a person who dons the mask of a friend while concealing ulterior motives. They might pretend to be your confidant and ally, yet behind that façade, they harbor feelings of competition, jealousy, or even ill will. The word "frenemy" is a portmanteau of "friend" and "enemy," encapsulating the notion that not all people who call themselves friends have your best interests at heart.

Distinguishing between true friends and frenemies is an essential life skill. Frenemies are notorious for disguising insults as compliments. They might say something like, "You look pretty today, considering how you usually look," subtly undermining your self-esteem.

Frenemies excel at passive-aggressiveness. They maintain a facade of friendliness while subtly undermining you with their words or actions. It's as if they're being nice on the surface but planting seeds of doubt beneath. Frenemies might not actively support your efforts and, in some cases, they'll work against your success. This can manifest as spreading rumors about you, sabotaging your opportunities, or belittling your achievements.

Healthy competition among friends can be motivating, but frenemies take it to extremes. They're constantly comparing themselves to you, seeking ways to outdo you or make you feel inadequate.

Frenemies often put on a public facade of friendship but behave differently in private. They may engage in gossip, betray your trust, or display two-faced behavior, sowing seeds of mistrust.

Frenemies are skilled in the art of emotional manipulation. They can switch between being sweet and caring one moment and cold and distant the next, leaving you off balance and questioning your own actions.

True friends celebrate your achievements and offer genuine support. In contrast, frenemies may feel jealous or attempt to downplay your accomplishments. They might even try to steal your spotlight.

Your true friends will uplift you and genuinely care about your well-being, offering a positive and nurturing environment for your personal growth and happiness.

BE THE BOSS: STAND UP FOR YOURSELF

In the age of the internet, peer pressure isn't confined to in-person interactions; it's a lurking menace in social media circles, too. It's like an invisible force that subtly influences your decisions, from the clothes you wear to the content you post, and it can even challenge your core beliefs. In this section, we will navigate the world of digital peer pressure, shedding light on its influence and equipping you with strategies to combat it effectively, whether it occurs in the digital realm or the real world.

Digital peer pressure is a formidable adversary. It manifests in the form of trends, comments, and "likes" on social media platforms. These platforms constantly bombard you with curated content, often giving you a distorted view of reality. As a result, you may find yourself caught in a whirlwind of comparison, self-doubt, and the relentless pressure to conform to what seems "normal" online.

The desire for online validation, in the form of likes, comments, and followers, can sometimes overshadow your authenticity. You may post content not because it represents your true self, but because it's what you believe others want to see.

To stand strong against digital peer pressure, it's crucial to recognize its presence. Here are some signs that might indicate you're experiencing digital peer pressure:

- **Comparison game:** You're constantly comparing your life, looks, achievements, or online popularity to what you see on your social media feeds, leading to feelings of inadequacy or discontent.
- **Seeking validation:** You find yourself posting content primarily for the purpose of receiving validation from your online peers. The number of likes and comments becomes a measure of your self-worth.
- **Changing opinions:** You start to shift your beliefs, values, or stances on various issues to align with the

popular online narrative, even if it doesn't genuinely reflect your own perspective.

- **Online vs. real self:** Your online persona becomes drastically different from who you are in real life. This divide between your digital identity and your true self can lead to a sense of disconnection.

## ACTIVITY: ROLE-PLAY—WHAT WOULD YOU DO?

Peer pressure can be an unexpected challenge, leaving you momentarily uncertain of how to respond. Role-playing is a fantastic way to prepare for these situations, enabling you to practice and build confidence in your decision-making. In this activity, we will explore various scenarios where peer pressure from friends and frenemies may come into play. You'll be provided with responses and an understanding of the psychology behind them, empowering you to handle such situations effectively.

### Scenario 1: Fashion Frenzy

Situation: You and your friends are getting ready for a night out. They insist that you wear an outfit you're not comfortable in.

### Response 1—The Assertive Approach

With a confident tone, you respond, "I appreciate the suggestion, but I'm going to wear what makes me feel comfortable and confident. I hope you can understand that."

This response reflects assertiveness, demonstrating self-assuredness. It's an effective way to stand your ground without creating confrontation. It conveys that you value your friends' input but that you prioritize your comfort and self-expression.

**Response 2—The Humorous Deflection**

You playfully respond, "You really think I'd look good in that? I admire your fashion sense, but I think I'll stick to what suits my style best."

Using humor to deflect the pressure can lighten the situation and ease any tension. It allows you to maintain your boundaries while emphasizing that it's a matter of personal style preference.

**Response 3—The Compromise**

You say, "I can see why you like that outfit, but how about we meet in the middle? I'll wear something that's a bit different but still within my comfort zone."

This response shows that you're open to considering their input and willing to meet them halfway. It's a diplomatic way to assert your own preferences while valuing your friends' opinions.

### *Scenario 2: Risky Business*

Situation: Your friends pressure you to do something you're not comfortable with, like trying an illicit substance.

**Response 1—The Firm Refusal**

You firmly state, "No, I'm not comfortable with that. I'm going to pass."

A clear and direct refusal helps establish your boundaries. It communicates that you've thought about your decision and won't be swayed by peer pressure. It also emphasizes that your well-being is your priority.

**Response 2—The Diversion Tactic**

You say, "I appreciate the offer, but I've got other plans for the night. Let's catch up later."

Using a diversion tactic, you effectively redirect the focus away from the pressure-inducing situation. This response allows you to maintain your boundaries and avoid direct confrontation while also ensuring your well-being.

**Response 3—The Educated Response**

You respond, "I've read a lot about the risks associated with that, and I'd rather not take any chances with my health."

The educated response involves sharing information that demonstrates you've considered the situation carefully. It emphasizes your commitment to your well-being while subtly encouraging your friends to think about their choices as well. This response can sometimes prompt a more informed discussion about the potential consequences of their actions and encourage responsible decision-making.

AFFIRMATIONS SECTION: ARMOR OF WORDS

Your thoughts possess the transformative ability to mold your reality, and the significance of your self-dialogue cannot be underestimated. Affirmations are a protective shield of positivity, safeguarding your self-esteem and self-worth, especially in peer pressure. In this segment, we delve into the profound influence of self-talk and affirmations in cultivating mental resilience when confronted with peer pressure.

Positive affirmations are concise and uplifting statements you can recite daily and they are potent instruments for reshaping your thought patterns and fostering a more favorable self-perception. By embracing self-affirmation, you empower yourself to elevate your self-esteem, self-worth, and self-assuredness.

When confronted with peer pressure, your internal discourse becomes a pivotal factor in weakening or bolstering your determination. Negative self-talk possesses the potential to undermine your self-esteem, rendering you more susceptible to the influence of peer pressure. Conversely, positive self-talk and affirmations function as a mental bulwark, fortifying your resistance against external pressures.

**Affirmations for Mental Resilience**

- "I am enough just as I am."
- "I value and respect myself."
- "I am strong and confident in my choices."

- "I trust my instincts and make decisions that align with my values."
- "I am not defined by the opinions of others."
- "I choose authenticity over conformity."
- "I am proud of my individuality."
- "I am resilient in the face of peer pressure."
- "I believe in my ability to stand up for what I believe in."
- "I am the captain of my own ship, and I steer it with confidence."

These affirmations are like a mental suit of armor. By repeating them daily, you reinforce your self-esteem, boost your self-worth, and strengthen your mental resilience. They remind you of your intrinsic value and the importance of staying true to yourself, even in the face of peer pressure. In the chapters ahead, we will delve deeper into strategies for maintaining your authenticity and navigating the complexities of friendships and peer dynamics.

# 3

# HOW SOCIAL MEDIA CAN AFFECT YOUR EMOTIONAL HEALTH

In this digital age, where every swipe and scroll reveals a piece of our lives, social media has become the canvas where we paint our stories, shape our identities, and connect with the world. It's like a world where the lines between reality and the digital realm often blend, and it can sometimes affect our self-esteem and self-image.

We are peeling back the layers of the social media story to uncover the truths hidden beneath. Social media isn't just a place to share; it's like a magic mirror reflecting how we see our lives and others. Sometimes, it can warp our view of reality, influence our mental well-being, and shape our beliefs.

After all, "social media has inserted itself between each of us and our daily experiences, moderating and manipulating the information we receive about our society" (Rosenberg, 2022, para. 17). The algorithms behind the platforms curate customized content for us, and sometimes, we don't even realize it's happening.

## FAKE PERFECTION: HOW SOCIAL MEDIA TRICKS YOU

Welcome to the fabulous world of social media, where reality gets a makeover, and perfection is just a filter away. It's like a place where everyone has the perfect hair day, an unending vacation, and a lifetime supply of gourmet meals. But guess what? There's a little more to this picture than meets the eye.

Understand this:

- Every photo is a work of art.
- Every caption is carefully crafted.
- Every moment is carefully handpicked for its "Instagrammability."

In social media, we are talking radiant smiles, flawless skin, exotic destinations, and fancier food than the Buckingham Palace tea party. It's like living in a non-stop glam-fest.

Well, hold onto your selfie stick because here comes the plot twist: life, for most people, isn't like that. It's more like a roller coaster of ups, downs, and everything. But on social media, it's all about maintaining appearances and filtering out the ordinary (sometimes the chaotic).

"All this filtered, picture-perfect living can mess with your mind. It sets the bar impossibly high and might even make you feel like your life is a bit, well, ordinary. But here's the secret: that's not the whole story" (Hovey, 2019, para 2).

In the world of social media, everyone else is leading a life filled with never-ending adventure, always surrounded by friends, and constantly achieving success. The carefully curated images and stories shared on these platforms can create a sense of inadequacy for those who believe they fall short of these seemingly perfect lives. The pressure to match these idealized versions of reality can be overwhelming.

When we dig beneath the surface of social media, we begin to understand the complexities that lie beneath. People's online personas often showcase only the highlights of their lives, the moments of success, and the meticulously polished experiences. However, social media doesn't always reflect the full range of human experiences, such as the struggles with mental health, the quiet nights spent at home, or the financial challenges that many of us face. It is a highly selective portrayal, leading to distorted perceptions of what a perfect life should be. According to Thomas (2016):

> The long-term psychological impact of social media on individuals and their sense of 'self' remains to be seen. But there is one thing we do know. Our daily lives have been digitized and tracked in metrics. Our real selves have split into online avatars, profile pictures, and status updates. And while social media sites like Facebook, Twitter, and LinkedIn are powerful tools that have the potential to build communities, connect relatives in far-flung places, leverage careers, and even elect presidents

of the U.S., they are also unleashing myriad complex
psychological issues that have altered our collective
sense of reality. (para 6)

Social media has transformed the way we interact with one
another and has woven itself into the fabric of our daily lives. It
has brought both unprecedented connectivity and unforeseen
psychological challenges. As we navigate this digital landscape,
it's important to be mindful of the potential impact it can have
on our self-esteem and our perception of reality.

Armed with this knowledge, you can take charge of your digital
experience and wander the digital jungle with a pinch of
authenticity, a dash of humor, and a lot of self-acceptance.
Remember that the images and stories you encounter online
represent just one facet of a person's life, and the reality behind
the screen is often far more complex and relatable than it
appears. Embrace the uniqueness of your journey and find a
balance between the digital and the real world that works
for you.

### Photo Filters: The Digital Makeup Artists

Picture photo filters as your very own makeup artist but for
your pictures. These incredible filters have the power to turn a
regular selfie into a work of art. They can tweak colors,
enhance lighting, and give your skin a radiant, otherworldly
glow. It's like waving a digital wand that can make you look like
a superstar, even on a just-rolled-out-of-bed kind of day.

Now, filters can do wonders for your photos, no doubt about it. However, it's important to remember that they can also create unrealistic beauty standards. When you see images that have been polished and perfected with filters, it's easy to forget that behind those images are real people with real imperfections. So, while filters are fantastic for adding a dash of enchantment to your images, don't forget that your natural beauty is something to be celebrated.

### Selective Posting: The Highlight Reel Effect

You probably have a friend who seems to live a life straight out of a Hollywood blockbuster, right? Their social media is a constant stream of fantastic adventures, delectable meals, and glittering moments. That's the magic of selective posting. It's like showcasing only the shiniest gems in your treasure trove while keeping the less dazzling bits hidden away.

Now, this approach can make your social media profile look like a box office hit, but it can also stir up feelings of inadequacy for those watching. When you're comparing your everyday life to someone's carefully curated highlight reel, it's like comparing your rough draft to their finished novel. It's not a fair contest. Your everyday life, complete with its ups and downs, is a real masterpiece on its own.

### Self-Presentation Strategies: Crafting the Digital You

In social media, many individuals take their online presence incredibly seriously. They transform into digital architects, meticulously editing their photos as if crafting a digital master-piece, arranging scenes as though they're the directors of block-buster films, and even spinning elaborate tales to add a dash of drama to their virtual lives. It's all about becoming the protago-nist of your digital narrative and shaping an image that mirrors your aspirations.

While curating your digital persona can be immensely enjoy-able, it's vital to maintain sight of your genuine, authentic self. The real you, complete with your idiosyncrasies, quirks, and everyday moments, is an enthralling story in its own right. You don't need to don the director's hat for a Hollywood block-buster in the digital realm. It's your unique, unscripted moments that contain the real magic.

In today's digital age, it's essential to recognize that carefully edited online personas can serve as a smoke screen, masking profound issues like anxiety and depression. While portraying an idealized version of yourself online isn't inherently problem-atic, it's worth noting that, as Dr. Jill Emanuele from the Child Mind Institute points out, social media can exacerbate chal-lenging situations (Jacobson, 2022). Teens who have meticu-lously crafted idealized online personas may eventually grapple with frustration and depression stemming from the disparity between their online facade and their true selves.

The impact of beauty filters and idealized beauty standards on mental health is another critical consideration. Exposure to images enhanced by beauty filters can increase social compar-ison and body image concerns, affecting self-esteem and body satisfaction. Children and teens need to understand that these filters may perpetuate problematic ideals and biases like colorism, ageism, and anti-fat bias (Evans, 2021).

It's crucial to remember that these filters often express stereo-typically binary masculine and feminine characteristics (Evans, 2021). In reality, there is a vast spectrum of beauty and identity, and these filters don't define what's attractive or valid.

So, while embracing your creative side in the digital world is undoubtedly exciting, always keep in mind that your true, authentic self is a captivating story in itself. You don't need a scripted, idealized version of your life to shine online; your everyday, unfiltered moments are where the real enchantment resides.

## FROM SCROLLING TO STRESSING: IT'S A THING

Now, let's journey deeper into the heart of the digital realm, where emotions can take you on quite a ride. Scrolling through social media is not all unicorns and rainbows; it's more like a rollercoaster of feelings that can leave your head spinning. From FOMO to anxiety, social media can be a whirlwind of emotions, and it's crucial to understand how it affects your mental well-being.

### The FOMO Phenomenon: Fear of Missing Out

FOMO, or the Fear of Missing Out, isn't a novel concept. Coined back in 1996 and officially recognized by the Oxford English Dictionary in 2013, it's precisely what it sounds like: the nagging fear or anxiety that somewhere, something interesting or thrilling is happening without your presence (Weiss, 2022, para 2). It's akin to being stuck watching the tantalizing trailer of everyone else's lives while you wonder why your own doesn't feel like a Hollywood blockbuster. That little voice in your head persistently questions, "Why am I not there?"

For many teenagers, FOMO can become an all-consuming concern, leading to anxiety and a diminished sense of self, resulting in mental, social, and physical consequences (Weiss, 2022). Picture this scenario: you're scrolling through your social media feed, and it seems like all your friends are partying the night away at an event you weren't invited to or having a blast at a gathering you couldn't attend. It's like witnessing everyone else enjoy the coolest theme park while you're stuck at home, wondering what you're missing.

Social media, in particular, can serve as a potent trigger for FOMO. Research from the 2015 National Stress and Well-Being in Australia Survey found that heavy teenage social media users might feel that their relationships are stronger (Weiss, 2022). However, the same research revealed that these teens are also less likely to feel burnt out, less likely to experience a sense of missing out, and less preoccupied with the number of "likes" on their posts when they reduce their time spent on social media. The virtual world serves as a constant reminder of the exciting happenings you're not a part of.

Adolescents are particularly susceptible to the development of FOMO through social media. It's not solely tied to individual characteristics but is also influenced by the family environment, including family structure, parental relationship quality, and parenting style (Bloemen & De Coninck, 2020). Family context and relationships play a substantial role in an adolescent's experience of FOMO. For instance, being part of a non-intact family, the parenting style of fathers, and the perceived quality of relationships with parents can either protect against or elevate the risk of FOMO. This highlights the significance of the family setting in shaping an adolescent's perception of missing out.

Furthermore, the constant connection that mobile and social media offer can fuel FOMO, particularly among adolescents. The allure of staying perpetually online, coupled with the exponential growth of social media, makes it an integral part of the lives of many youngsters. They rely on these platforms for communication, information, and even emotional self-regulation (Bloemen & De Coninck, 2020). This increased dependence raises concerns about the impact of excessive social media use on the well-being and development of children and adolescents, both in the short and long term.

Research has also highlighted the overlap between FOMO and internet addiction, emphasizing that FOMO can act as a mediator between the fulfillment of basic psychological needs, such as competence, personal independence, and social connectedness, and social media use (Bloemen & De Coninck, 2020). It's an emotional experience that arises when these essential psychological needs aren't met, and individuals turn to social media to stimulate their social connection and competence. As a result, people who experience FOMO are more likely to spend excessive time online, using social media as a platform to gather information about others.

So, FOMO isn't just a fleeting feeling. It's a tangible and potentially enduring concern, particularly in the digital age where constant connection and comparison are the norm. Striking a balance between staying informed about the world and nurturing your well-being and self-worth is the challenge. The digital age offers us many experiences and opportunities, but it's essential to remember that your self-worth isn't measured by the events you attend or the posts you make.

### The Anxiety Avalanche

In today's digital landscape, social media often resembles an unending popularity contest, which can be incredibly overwhelming for teenagers. Picture it like being thrust onto a grand virtual stage, where a relentless spotlight shines upon you, and the pressure to deliver a flawless performance never wanes.

Extensive research has shed light on a robust link between engaging with social media and teenage anxiety. It's like being caught in an eternal race, where the finish line continuously moves farther away, and your self-worth becomes inexorably tied to the number of virtual accolades you amass. The ceaseless comparisons to peers, the persistent fear of missing out on thrilling experiences, and the unwavering pursuit of validation through likes and comments combine to create a perfect storm of anxiety.

The emotional ramifications of social media are profound, demanding our earnest consideration. While the online world offers excitement and connections, it also harbors enticing yet unattainable ideals. In the words of Whyte (2021, para 16), "Teens are subjected to a lot of different pressures from social media, but the connection between social media and teen anxiety is not as simple as you may think. For teens who are already struggling with insecurities, social media can trigger feelings of anxiety and pressure to get likes and comments on their posts."

Furthermore, as highlighted by Whyte (2021, para 20), presenting an idealized "highlight reel" on social media can lead to feelings of inadequacy, especially for those whose lives may not be as glamorous. The anxiety stemming from the perceived lack of excitement in one's life is a tangible concern: "Teens who don't have exciting photos can feel anxious that their life isn't good enough or that others will see that they are lacking in status."

Additionally, the pursuit of boosting one's "social currency" in the digital realm, as noted by Whyte (2021, para 21), can be a significant source of anxiety induced by social media. This refers to a user's ability to influence others, promote products, or cultivate a brand that attracts a substantial following. The relentless quest for social currency can become a source of persistent stress.

The negative consequences of social media extend beyond self-esteem and validation. Online harassment and cyberbullying, as underlined by Whyte (2021), are among the most dangerous effects of social media on teen stress. The pervasive nature of these issues, often from strangers worldwide, amplifies the emotional turmoil adolescents can experience in the digital sphere.

Interestingly, as Shafer (2017) points out, experts have noticed a surge in sleeplessness, loneliness, worry, and dependence among teenagers in the era of smartphones and social media. One study even found that the duration of electronic device usage is significantly linked to suicide risk factors. Adolescents who spend more time on their devices are at a higher risk, highlighting the potential grave consequences of excessive screen time.

The relationship between anxiety and social media is multifaceted, as Shafer (2017) emphasizes. It's not a simple one-way street where social media causes stress. Factors such as pre-existing depression and anxiety may lead to increased social media use, and there could be unknown variables at play, such as academic pressures or economic concerns. Moreover, contemporary teens may be more open about their mental health concerns than previous generations.

It's essential to navigate the digital world with mindfulness. Social media is like standing on a virtual stage with a relentless spotlight, but we must remember that our self-worth should not be defined by the number of virtual trophies we collect. Being ourselves and not letting social media dictate our value is crucial in this digital age.

## DON'T LET LIKES DEFINE YOU

In the captivating world of social media, where metrics like likes, followers, and comments reign supreme, it's all too easy to let these numbers become the measure of your self-worth. But, my dear reader, it's imperative to understand that these modern-day yardsticks do not and should not define your true value. Let's dive deeper into why this reliance on social media metrics can be problematic and discover alternative measures of self-worth deeply rooted in intrinsic values.

Social media has created a metric trap where self-esteem is directly linked to the numbers that appear beneath your posts. The more likes you accumulate, the higher your follower count, the more you feel validated and accepted. It's like having an applause meter that measures your self-worth based on the approval you receive from others.

The problem with this approach is that it transforms self-esteem into a numbers game. It can lead to a constant quest for external validation, where your mood and self-worth are tied to every notification and validation-seeking post. Imagine waking up each morning and immediately checking your latest post to see how many likes it's garnered. If the number is high, you experience a sense of delight; if it's low, you're disappointed. It's like living on an emotional rollercoaster controlled by a social media algorithm.

*Intrinsic Value: What Really Matters*

Your true worth extends far beyond the numbers on your social media profile. It's not about the likes you receive or the number of followers you've amassed; it's about the qualities that make you uniquely you. Think about your kindness, your creativity, your ability to make people smile, and your resilience in the face of adversity—these are the qualities that genuinely define your self-worth.

Intrinsic values, such as being a good friend, pursuing your passions, learning and growing, and making a positive impact on the world, are infinitely more meaningful than any number of likes or followers. Imagine the satisfaction of creating something beautiful, the joy of helping someone in need, or the pride of mastering a new skill. These moments are the ones that genuinely enrich your life and make it worth living.

## MAKE YOUR FEED A HAPPY PLACE

Imagine your social media feed as a vibrant garden, with the content and people you follow as the seeds you plant. Just as you carefully select flowers and plants to create a beautiful and peaceful garden, your choices in curating your online experience can have a significant impact on your mental well-being and self-image. Let's dive into how your decisions about what you see online can either uplift your spirits or leave you feeling drained and explore practical strategies to ensure your digital space becomes a source of joy.

Like you'd choose flowers that brighten your garden, follow accounts that inspire, educate, and motivate you. Seek out content creators who share your interests, passions, and dreams. Whether it's a fitness enthusiast demonstrating workout routines or an artist showcasing their creations, opt for accounts that resonate with you.

In your garden, you would want to keep the beauty of your flowers distinct from weeds. Similarly, if you come across accounts that consistently make you feel bad about yourself or promote negativity, it's time to remove them from your digital space. This could include influencers who perpetuate unrealistic beauty standards, individuals who engage in cyberbullying, or anyone whose content doesn't align with your values.

Just like a community of like-minded gardening enthusiasts can help your plants flourish, connect with individuals who uplift and support you online. Engage in conversations and interactions that encourage personal growth and positive connections.

Sometimes, online interactions can be like unexpected storms in your garden. If you encounter negative comments or messages, remember that you can choose how you respond. Disengage from toxic conversations, and don't hesitate to block or report users who engage in harmful behavior.

By thoughtfully curating your social media experience, you can transform your digital space into a source of positivity and inspiration. It's about creating a digital environment that not only reflects your interests and passions but also nurtures your self-worth and happiness. Your social media can reflect your unique personality, and with the right choices, it can become a place where you truly bloom and flourish.

## ACTIVITY: SOCIAL MEDIA DETOX PLAN

Are you ready to embark on a journey of self-discovery and reconnection with the real world? Social media can be both a wonderful tool for connection and a source of stress, and this Social Media Detox Plan is designed to help you take a break from the digital realm and re-evaluate its role in your life.

Before you begin your detox, it's important to identify your objectives. Ask yourself what you hope to achieve during this break. Is it to reduce screen time, boost your self-esteem, find more meaningful ways to spend your time, or take a breather from the digital world? Knowing your goals will give your detox a clear purpose and help keep you motivated.

The next step is to decide how long you want your detox to last. Detox durations vary widely, from a weekend to a week or up to a month. Pick a duration that aligns with your goals and comfort level. If you're new to the idea of a social media detox, starting with a shorter period might be a good idea.

Now that you've set your goals and chosen your detox duration, let your online friends and followers know about your plans. A simple post or message explaining that you'll be taking a break can set the right expectations and reduce the temptation to check in during detox. It's also a considerate way to maintain your online relationships.

To make your detox easier, remove the social media app icons from your phone's home screen. The "out of sight, out of mind" principle applies here. When you don't see those familiar app icons every time you unlock your phone, you're less likely to open them mindlessly.

Taking control of your notifications is essential for a successful detox. Go through your phone's settings and turn off notifications for social media apps. This will prevent your device from constantly vying for your attention and help you focus on other activities.

Without social media, you'll suddenly find yourself with extra time. Now is the perfect opportunity to consider how you'd like to spend it. Consider activities you genuinely enjoy or new things you've been curious to explore. You could read a book, start a journal, take up a new hobby, or spend quality time with loved ones.

During your detox, take time to reflect on how you feel without social media. Are you less stressed, more present, or happier? How are your interactions with friends and family evolving? Jot down your thoughts and emotions in a journal to capture your experiences. Use this time to reconnect with yourself and your surroundings.

Once your detox period is over, it's time for a thorough self-assessment. What did you learn about yourself and your relationship with social media during the detox? Did you discover any unhealthy habits, or did you realize the positive aspects of social media? Use this introspection to decide how to incorporate these insights into your digital life moving forward.

Based on your reflections and learnings, set new boundaries for your social media use. This could involve limiting your screen time, following more positive and inspirational accounts, or using certain platforms exclusively for specific purposes (e.g., Instagram for artistic inspiration). These boundaries should align with your goals and help you maintain a healthy and balanced digital life.

You've completed your social media detox, and that's a remarkable achievement! Celebrate your journey and the self-discovery you've made. Reward yourself with something you enjoy, whether it's a cozy movie night, a favorite treat, or an outing to a place you love.

## AFFIRMATIONS SECTION: DIGITAL SHIELD

The digital world, with its myriad social media platforms, holds an intricate tapestry of opportunities and challenges. On one hand, it connects us, provides us with information, and offers a platform to express ourselves. On the other hand, it can expose us to unrealistic standards, foster self-doubt, and disrupt our self-esteem.

But fear not, for you possess a secret weapon in this digital battlefield: affirmations. These simple yet potent statements can fortify your mental armor, acting as a digital shield to protect you from the toxicity that sometimes swirls around the online world.

Life in the digital age can be filled with ups and downs, but affirmations help you bounce back from setbacks. They remind you of your inner strength and your ability to overcome challenges, no matter how daunting they may seem. Affirmations transform you into a digital warrior, resilient in adversity. Affirmations act as your inner defenders, combating negativity with positivity and self-compassion. They remind you to treat yourself kindly, just as you would a dear friend.

- "I am more than the sum of my likes and comments. My worth goes beyond online validation."
- "I choose to focus on my own journey, not someone else's highlight reel."
- "I am in control of my digital experience. I decide what I see and engage with."
- "I celebrate my uniqueness and the beauty of my imperfections."
- "I use social media to inspire and be inspired, not to compare and despair."
- "I am the author of my own story, and I share it with intention and authenticity."
- "I am resilient. I can overcome any digital challenges and emerge stronger."
- "I prioritize real-world connections and experiences over virtual ones."
- "I use social media as a tool for learning, growth, and connection."
- "I am mindful of the content I consume, and I choose what brings me joy and positivity."

# 4

# GLOW UP FROM THE INSIDE— YOU'RE ALREADY A 10/10!

In a world that often magnifies our flaws and insecurities, this is a gentle reminder that you deserve love and admiration just as you are. You will soon be able to craft self-affirmations that celebrate both your inner and outer beauty, paving the way for a profound transformation of self-love.

In the melodious words of Lady Gaga, "I'm beautiful in my way 'cause God makes no mistakes." So, let's get ready to learn how to truly appreciate the unique beauty that each one of us possesses.

In a world that often emphasizes perfection and external standards, it's crucial to remember that beauty comes in countless forms. Each of us is a masterpiece in our own right, with a unique blend of qualities and traits that make us who we are.

## WHAT MAKES YOU TRULY STUNNING?

Welcome to a world where Instagram filters, perfect selfies, and those "ideal" beauty standards seem everywhere. It's like a never-ending beauty contest that sometimes makes us question our awesomeness. But guess what? It's time to break free from these beauty myths and discover the magic inside you.

You know, everyone talks about beauty like it's just about having the perfect body shape, and it's easy to get frustrated when we can't match up to those impossible standards (Edubirdie, 2022). But here's the scoop: Beauty isn't just about your looks. It's also about how you feel about yourself.

"Beauty can be defined as the personal satisfaction of looking good about various stereotypes that society has established" (Edubirdie, 2022, para. 3). This means beauty is personal. It doesn't have to fit anyone else's idea of perfection. It's about what makes you feel confident and happy.

Let's break free from the confines of societal expectations and redefine beauty on our terms. Rather than molding ourselves into someone else's image for the sake of social media validation, let's revel in the beauty of authenticity and self-expression.

Beauty standards, as Raaziya (2023) points out, often dictate what is considered attractive or handsome based on superficial criteria like skin, hair, and body appearance. But here's the truth: These standards are merely external measurements and do not encompass the richness of who we are. We are not confined to the narrow definitions set by society.

It's essential to recognize that beauty extends far beyond a number on a scale or conforming to an unrealistic set of physical features, as highlighted by Kassir (2021). True beauty is not about fitting into a predetermined mold; it's about embracing the essence of who you are. Your uniqueness, kindness, and self-confidence are the elements that make you genuinely beautiful.

Let's embark on a beauty revolution that celebrates individuality! It's time to embrace and showcase the beauty of your true self, free from the constraints of someone else's standards. Beauty lies in your authenticity, in the quirks that make you, you. Your confidence radiates from within, illuminating your unique qualities and making you truly beautiful.

So, let's toss aside the notion of copying someone else's style or conforming to a specific shape. Instead, let's celebrate the beauty that each individual brings to the table. It's time to love and appreciate yourself for who you are, allowing your true beauty to shine brightly. This is a call to embrace the real you, to be proud of your uniqueness, and to let your authenticity be the true measure of your beauty. Join the movement, and let your beauty revolution begin!

Challenge beauty standards by educating those around you. Spark conversations with friends, family, and classmates about the unrealistic expectations placed on individuals, and share the message that beauty is diverse. Encourage open dialogue about self-acceptance and the importance of embracing differences.

## *Deconstructing Society's Beauty Definitions*

You have probably noticed that society has this knack for telling us what's beautiful and what's not. From magazines to ads to our social media feeds, they paint a picture of beauty that often doesn't match the incredible diversity of how people look. They've created this checklist of what it takes to be beautiful.

"Often, what we truly perceive as beautiful is not what is traditionally externally pleasing to the eye. We recognize people as beautiful when being around them makes us feel good. We see them beneath their surface" (Leinwand, 2017, para 5). Beauty isn't just skin deep. It's what's inside that counts. It's how someone makes you feel, their kindness, and how they treat others.

According to Jines (2017):

> Society sets these expectations of beauty on girls at such a young age but does not recognize that more than just outward appearance makes a person beautiful. No one was created the same, so there should not be one idea of what beauty is. (Para 7)

So why does society try to squeeze us into one beauty mold when we're all so wonderfully different? It's like trying to fit a round peg into a square hole.

These so-called beauty standards can be harmful. They make us believe there's only one way to be beautiful: one specific body type, shade of skin, or facial features. But here's the truth:

There's no one-size-fits-all definition of beauty. It's like trying to fit an entire rainbow into just one color.

When we dig deeper into these standards, we find they are built on myths and misconceptions. Pursuing these ideals can be downright exhausting, and the pressure to fit within these standards can take a toll on our self-esteem and mental well-being.

But guess what? You don't have to chase these beauty myths. You are amazing, just the way you are. You have a unique beauty that shines from within. It's your quirks, your passions, your kindness, and your confidence that make you beautiful. So, let's rewrite the beauty standards. Let's celebrate our differences and recognize that beauty is about being yourself and spreading positivity. Because true beauty is found in your heart and how you treat others.

### *Debunking Beauty Myths*

It's time to challenge these myths and question their legitimacy. Beauty is not one-size-fits-all, nor is it confined to external appearances alone. It's a multifaceted gem with numerous facets, and how you reflect its brilliance is unique to you.

### Myth 1: Beauty Equals Perfection

Contrary to society's portrayal, beauty is not synonymous with flawlessness. In fact, imperfections are the brushstrokes that paint the canvas of our uniqueness and authenticity. They are the storytellers of our experiences, growth, and resilience. True beauty lies in embracing and celebrating these imperfections as the elements that make us real and extraordinary.

**Myth 2: Beauty is All About Looks**

True beauty surpasses the superficial confines of physical appearances. It encompasses the depths of kindness, the warmth of empathy, the glow of intelligence, and the resilience that resides within. Your actions, the way you treat others, and your ability to face challenges head-on contribute to a stunning beauty that goes beyond mere looks.

**Myth 3: Beauty is Static**

Beauty is a dynamic force that evolves and transforms with time. It's influenced by your personality, interests, passions, and your capacity to adapt to life's ever-changing landscapes. Your beauty is not a stagnant pond but a flowing river shaped by the currents of your experiences and the growth that accompanies them.

**Myth 4: Beauty is One-Size-Fits-All**

The true beauty of beauty lies in its diversity. There's no universal standard that applies to everyone. What one person finds beautiful may differ from another, and that's not only acceptable but also wonderful. Embracing this diversity allows us to appreciate the richness of beauty in all its forms.

Now, as we clear away these misconceptions, we can recognize that beauty reflects your inner light. It shines through your actions, your character, and your uniqueness. It's about embracing your individuality and acknowledging that you are stunning, just as you are, without trying to fit into someone else's mold.

As we journey further into this chapter, we'll explore the various facets of your inner beauty and learn to celebrate them. We'll uncover the qualities that make you truly stunning, and you will discover that your authentic self is a work of art, unparalleled and breathtaking.

## STOP STRESSING OVER YOUR REFLECTION

In a world where unrealistic beauty standards are omnipresent, it's all too common to feel like we don't measure up. We've all been there, scrutinizing ourselves in the mirror, zeroing in on minor imperfections, and trying to conceal them with makeup or avoiding social situations altogether. It's like a never-ending battle with our reflection.

Raaziya (2023) highlights that approximately two percent of the population grapples with body dysmorphia, a mental health disorder that often takes root in the fertile soil of self-disappointment. Those affected by it believe their appearance is riddled with flaws, far more than anyone else's. It's a struggle that particularly hits teenagers and young adults, affecting both males and females equally. It's essential to recognize that sometimes these flaws exist only in our imagination.

Statistics on eating disorders are startling. They have spiked from 3.4% to 7.8%, with approximately 70 million people worldwide struggling with these disorders. And here's the kicker: Societal standards and the ever-influential impact of social media are contributing factors. The pressure to conform to these standards pushes people to transform themselves, leading to dangerous relationships with food (Raaziya, 2023).

Moreover, the toll on mental health is evident in the statistics on suicidal thoughts due to body image. About 10% of women have self-harmed due to body dissatisfaction, and approximately 13% of adults have experienced suicidal thoughts and feelings after prolonged distress related to body image issues (Raaziya, 2023).

We all have moments when we question ourselves, our worth, and our appearance. It's a part of being human. But what can we do about it?

According to Wooll (2022), cultivating self-awareness is key. It's about taking a step back and evaluating how we react to challenges and opportunities, especially when we need to work independently. When those waves of self-doubt wash over us, taking a deep breath and self-reflection can be a game-changer.

It's important to note that self-criticism isn't inherently bad. It can serve as a constructive tool when used proactively. We can examine our decisions and behaviors, using self-critique to make positive changes. But it becomes problematic when it leads us to avoid things and self-sabotage our own experiences (Gulotta, 2022).

Ultimately, self-criticism can be a double-edged sword. While it can motivate us to grow and improve, it can also become a heavy burden, weighing down our self-esteem and harming our relationships with others (Gulotta, 2022). So, let's explore ways to use self-awareness as a tool for growth and challenge the destructive self-criticism that can erode our self-esteem. You are worth so much more than the negative thoughts that sometimes hold you back.

## *The Psychology of Self-Criticism*

Self-criticism, especially in physical appearance, is a complex psychological puzzle. At its heart lies the "inner critic"—a voice within us that constantly evaluates, judges, and critiques our actions, choices, and, yes, even our physical selves. Regarding our looks, this inner critic can become particularly relentless, honing in on what it sees as flaws or inadequacies.

The origins of this inner critic are multifaceted and deeply rooted in our psychology. Scientists have delved into the biological aspects, suggesting that our brains have a primitive "survivor brain" in the form of the brain stem, designed to focus on physical survival and the fight-or-flight response to danger. This part of our brain is hyper-aware of potential threats (Schaffner, 2020).

Interestingly, this inner critic wasn't always the negative force it can be today. Initially, its purpose was positive: ensuring our survival. This included identifying physical dangers in our environment and helping us make sense of complex psychological experiences (Schaffner, 2020).

Another facet of the inner critic's origin is closely tied to our early experiences. As children, we depended entirely on our parents for survival. Acknowledging any unfairness, cruelty, or incompetence in our caregivers was often too overwhelming. To protect ourselves, we turned this criticism inward, blaming ourselves for our difficulties (Schaffner, 2020).

The effects of this inner critic can be profound, impacting our emotional well-being and self-esteem. Even if we appear confident on the outside, the inner critic can plague us with feelings of shame, inadequacy, or guilt (GoodTherapy, 2015).

This inner critic, formed in our formative years when our survival depended on approval, tends to be rigid and simplistic. As we journey through life and encounter its complexities, the inner critic needs to evolve and adapt to navigate the subtleties and ambiguities of the adult world (Klammer, 2021).

So, what can we do to counteract this harsh inner critic? Self-affirmation and self-encouragement can be powerful tools. When that critical voice starts saying you are inferior or lacking, you can question its validity and choose to change its narrative. Most inner criticism stems from external social interactions, and by distancing yourself from it, you can begin the process of internal self-affirmation and self-encouragement.

In a world where external influences often amplify our self-criticism, it's crucial to recognize the origins of this inner critic and develop strategies to nurture a healthier and more positive self-perception. Remember, you are more than the judgments of your inner critic. Your worth extends far beyond the superficial, and you have the power to rewrite this narrative.

### Challenging Destructive Thought Patterns

We must acknowledge and challenge these destructive thought patterns to liberate ourselves from the relentless grip of self-criticism.

Imagine treating yourself with the same kindness, understanding, and empathy you would offer to a dear friend. When self-criticism rears its head, counter it with a dose of self-compassion. Remind yourself that you are human and nobody is perfect.

Mindfulness meditation is a valuable tool for becoming more aware of your thoughts and feelings without judgment. This practice lets you observe your inner critic without becoming entangled in its negativity.

Question their validity when you catch yourself entertaining self-critical thoughts about your appearance. Are these thoughts based on reality or distorted by self-doubt and societal pressures? Replace negative self-talk with more positive and realistic affirmations.

Instead of fixating on your perceived flaws, redirect your attention to your strengths and attributes that you are proud of. What are your talents, achievements, or qualities that make you unique and exceptional?

Comparison to others is a common trigger for self-criticism. It's crucial to remember that everyone is on a unique journey with their own set of challenges and imperfections. Instead of comparing yourself to others, celebrate the qualities that make you distinct and exceptional.

If self-criticism overwhelms your mental well-being, remember that you don't have to face it alone. Seek support from a trusted friend, family member, or mental health professional who can provide guidance, a listening ear, and a fresh perspective.

By incorporating these strategies into your daily life, you can gradually begin to reframe your self-critical thoughts and foster a healthier, more positive self-image. It's important to remember that your worth extends far beyond your physical appearance. You are a vibrant, multifaceted individual with unique qualities that make you extraordinary. Embrace self-compassion, and you will find that your reflection in the mirror becomes a source of self-love and acceptance.

## THE TOTAL YOU: BODY, MIND, AND SPIRIT

Beauty isn't just about what you see on the outside; it's about the incredible depth within. Think of it as a multi-faceted gem, with each facet representing a different part of you. Beauty goes beyond the surface and encompasses your physical health, emotional well-being, and the clarity of your mind.

Holistic therapy is like a treasure map that guides you to unlock the potential of this inner beauty. It's an adventure involving techniques like mindfulness meditation, visualization, and deep breathing exercises. These are the tools that help you navigate the sometimes-stormy waters of stress and anxiety. As you master these emotions, you will find a newfound sense of calm and strength.

But the journey doesn't stop there. Holistic therapy also encourages you to explore your passions, interests, and values. It's like discovering hidden treasures within yourself. This exploration often leads to a profound sense of purpose and fulfillment. As you connect with your inner self, your self-esteem and self-confidence will shine brighter.

So, beauty isn't just a one-dimensional concept. It's a masterpiece woven from your physical, emotional, and mental well-being threads. It's about embracing your unique symphony and understanding how each note contributes to your radiant beauty, far beyond what society may define. Your beauty is a holistic masterpiece that's uniquely yours.

### The Holistic Approach to Beauty

Taking a holistic approach to beauty means recognizing that these three aspects of well-being are intricately connected. Each facet contributes to the overall masterpiece that is you. Just as a painter blends different colors to create a harmonious composition, you must harmonize your body, mind, and spirit to create a balanced and beautiful life.

### Physical Well-Being

Physical well-being is the foundation upon which your inner and outer beauty stands. It is the outward manifestation of how you care for your body, reflecting not only in your appearance but also in your energy, vitality, and overall health.

### Nutrition

Show your body the love and care it deserves by embracing a balanced and wholesome diet. Infuse your meals with a vibrant palette of fruits, vegetables, lean proteins, and whole grains. Remember, nutrition isn't solely about outward appearance; it's a powerful means of ensuring you feel your best and safeguarding your overall well-being.

Now, let's delve into the details of this nourishing journey:

- Start your day with a hearty breakfast. Whole grains, such as whole-grain bread or brown rice, can provide the energy you need to kickstart your morning.
- Embrace a rainbow of fruits and vegetables. Aim to consume at least 2 cups of fruit and 2 ½ cups of vegetables daily, as these natural wonders contain essential vitamins, minerals, and nutrients.
- Your bones and teeth need some love, too. Ensure you are getting your daily dose of calcium, which can be found in foods like low-fat yogurt, milk, and fortified cereals.
- Protein is the building block of muscles and organs. Ensure you are consuming 5½ ounces of protein-rich foods each day, including lean meat, poultry, or fish.
- Iron is vital for growth, especially for boys during their substantial growth spurt. It can be found in lean beef, iron-fortified cereals and bread, beans, and leafy greens.
- Hydrate with water throughout the day. Limit sugary drinks and consume no more than 1 cup of 100% fruit juice daily.
- Don't forget vitamin D, which helps maintain healthy bones. Sources include dairy products, fortified beverages, salmon, mushrooms, and tuna.
- Potassium keeps your kidneys, heart, and muscles working efficiently. Seek it in foods like beans, potatoes, peppers, and fruits.
- Fiber plays a key role in regular bowel movements and feeling full. It also contributes to a lower risk of heart

and kidney diseases. You can find it in whole grains, fruits, and vegetables.

Remember, this nourishing journey isn't just about looking good; it's about feeling your best and nurturing your health from the inside out. Your body will thank you for the care and attention you provide through a balanced and colorful diet.

*Exercise*

Physical activity is more than just a means to an end; it's a continuous journey of self-care and well-being. The key is to discover an activity that truly resonates with you, whether dancing, hiking, swimming, or any other form of exercise. When you engage in regular physical activity, it's not just your physical health that reaps the benefits. Your mood also receives a delightful boost thanks to the release of those wonderful feel-good chemicals called endorphins.

It's important to remember that, as teenagers, your bodies undergo various changes, and regular exercise can be a powerful tool in embracing and adapting to these transformations. In addition to maintaining a healthy body shape, physical activity can enhance your mental health, contributing to greater self-confidence and emotional well-being.

Moreover, staying physically active helps you build and maintain a strong foundation of health. It's not only about preventing issues like cardiovascular diseases and obesity but also about developing habits that can set the stage for a healthy and active life.

So, whether you are a teenager or an adult, remember that physical activity is a lifelong journey, and the key is to find an activity you love. It's not about conforming to societal pressures; it's about embracing a healthy and active lifestyle that makes you feel your best.

## *Sleep*

Sleep is not just a nightly routine; it's your body's rejuvenating balm. It plays a pivotal role in your physical and mental development. Think of it as the time when your brain diligently processes information, consolidates memories, and recharges for the day ahead. To ensure you wake up refreshed and ready to take on the world, aim for a good 7–9 hours of quality sleep each night.

## Mental Clarity

Your mind is a powerful instrument that influences your perception of yourself and the world around you. Mental clarity is about maintaining a sharp and vibrant mind that allows you to think clearly and adapt to life's challenges.

To nurture your mental clarity, consider these practices:

- **Mindfulness exercises:** Mindfulness exercises, such as meditation, deep breathing, or even just moments of solitude, help you cultivate self-awareness, reduce stress, and enhance focus. A clear mind fosters a greater sense of peace and self-acceptance.

- **Positive self-talk:** Your inner dialogue profoundly impacts your self-esteem and self-worth. Replace self-criticism with self-encouragement and self-compassion. Celebrate your accomplishments and embrace your unique qualities.

## Emotional Stability

Emotional stability is the linchpin that perfectly aligns your inner and outer beauty. It equips you to manage your emotions, respond to stress, and build meaningful relationships. To nurture your emotional stability, consider these practices:

- **Emotional expression:** Emotions are a natural part of being human, and expressing them healthily is essential. Whether you use journaling, conversation, art, or music, ensure you have an outlet for your feelings. Emotional expression is a cornerstone of self-understanding.
- **Self-care:** Prioritize self-care activities that bring comfort and joy into your life. These may include taking a relaxing bath, reading a book, pursuing hobbies you love, or even just spending quality time with loved ones. Self-care is your bridge to inner serenity.
- **Seek support:** If you encounter overwhelming emotional challenges, remember that you are never alone in your journey. Reach out to a mental health professional, a trusted friend, or a family member who can offer support, guidance, and a fresh perspective.

This holistic approach to beauty encourages you to nurture your body, mind, and spirit, ensuring they thrive in harmony. True beauty transcends appearance boundaries, radiating from a vibrant body, a clear mind, and emotional equilibrium. Embrace this multifaceted beauty, and you will discover that the totality of your being is a masterpiece waiting to be unveiled.

## ACTIVITY: THE MIRROR CHALLENGE—A SELF-LOVE BOOST

The Mirror Challenge is a remarkable exercise crafted to uplift self-love and self-esteem. It invites you to turn your gaze inward, exploring your physical reflection and the depths of your emotions. It's a journey of self-discovery, and while it might initially feel a bit unfamiliar or even uncomfortable, over time, it becomes a potent instrument in nurturing a more profound and healthier connection with yourself.

You see, the foundation of self-esteem lies in recognizing your past achievements and successes. It's about celebrating your victories, regardless of whether others acknowledge them. This means it's your responsibility to be your biggest cheerleader and give yourself well-deserved pats when you succeed (Laundry, 2019).

The Mirror Challenge can be your path to not only seeing your reflection but also recognizing the countless triumphs that have shaped the person you are today. It's a powerful journey of self-recognition and self-appreciation.

**What You Will Need**

A mirror (full-length or handheld)

*Instructions*

Find a quiet, private space where you can have some alone time with your mirror. This exercise is about you, so ensure you won't be disturbed.

Stand in front of the mirror and take a few deep breaths to calm your mind. Relax and remember that this is your special time for self-love and self-acceptance.

Begin by focusing on your physical attributes. Look at your reflection and select a specific feature that you genuinely love. For example, you might say, "I love my bright, expressive eyes," or "I adore my radiant smile." Be genuine and specific in your affirmations.

Transition to your non-physical qualities. Think about your character and personality. Acknowledge and express appreciation for a trait that you love about yourself. This could be something like, "I appreciate my kindness and empathy," or "I love my sense of humor and creativity."

Now, look directly into your eyes in the mirror and, with sincerity, say, "I am enough, just as I am." This is a pivotal moment in the exercise, affirming your self-worth.

Express gratitude to yourself. Say, "Thank you for being the unique and wonderful person you are." This is a moment of self-recognition and appreciation.

Conclude the exercise with a smile directed at your reflection, and say, "I love you." Mean it with all your heart. This is an act of self-love that can be incredibly empowering.

**Tips**

Initially, you might feel self-conscious or even awkward during this exercise. That's completely okay. Self-love is a journey, and starting wherever you are is okay. The more you practice, the more comfortable it will become.

You can make this exercise a daily routine or do it as often as you like. The frequency is less important than the sincerity of your affirmations.

Don't worry if you start with just a few affirmations and gradually add more over time. The key is to be gentle and kind to yourself, appreciating all that makes you unique.

The Mirror Challenge is a beautiful way to connect with yourself, increase self-love, and boost your self-esteem. Your relationship with yourself is one of your most important relationships, and this exercise can help make it stronger and more positive. You are a remarkable and unique individual, and it's time to celebrate and appreciate that.

## AFFIRMATIONS AND JOURNAL PROMPTS: DAILY DECLARATIONS FOR UNVEILING YOUR INNER 10/10

This section offers you a collection of empowering affirmations and journal prompts to help you embrace your inner beauty and strength. Affirmations are like daily pep talks for your soul; journal prompts are tools for self-reflection and self-discovery.

## Physical Appearance Affirmations

- "I am beautiful just as I am."
- "I appreciate the uniqueness of my body and face."
- "I radiate confidence and inner beauty."
- "I am more than my physical appearance; I am a whole, extraordinary person."

## Intellectual Prowess Affirmations

- "I am intelligent and capable of learning and growing."
- "My mind is a wellspring of creativity and innovation."
- "I embrace challenges as opportunities to learn and excel."
- "I am constantly expanding my knowledge and wisdom."

## Emotional Well-Being Affirmations

- "I am worthy of love and respect from myself and others."
- "I trust my intuition and make decisions that serve my well-being."
- "I am resilient, and I can handle whatever life brings my way."
- "I control my emotions, and I choose positivity and happiness."

## *Journal Prompts*

- Reflect on a time when you felt truly confident in your appearance. What made you feel that way, and how can you recreate that feeling in your daily life?
- Describe an intellectual challenge you have faced recently. How did you handle it, and what did you learn from the experience?
- Write about a moment when you felt emotionally strong and resilient. What circumstances allowed you to tap into your emotional well-being, and how can you nurture that strength regularly?
- List three physical features you genuinely love about yourself and explain why.
- Recall a situation where your intelligence and knowledge played a significant role. How did it make you feel, and how can you celebrate your intellectual prowess more often?
- Consider a time when you managed your emotions effectively. What strategies did you use, and how can you apply them in daily life?
- Write a love letter to yourself, acknowledging your unique qualities and celebrating your inner and outer beauty.
- Reflect on the people who uplift and inspire you. How can you surround yourself with more positive influences in your life?
- What are the top three personal values that matter most to you? How can you honor and embody these values daily?

- Imagine yourself a year from now, overflowing with self-love and self-confidence. What actions will you have taken to make this transformation a reality?

Feel free to choose affirmations and journal prompts that resonate with you the most. Remember, self-love is a journey, and this is just one step on your path to unveiling your inner 10/10.

# 5

# HOW TO SLAY YOUR GRADES WITHOUT LOSING YOUR MIND

We are delving into the art of achieving academic excellence while safeguarding your mental health and well-being. It's all about finding the perfect balance between your studies and self-care.

As Michelle Obama wisely advises, "Don't ever make decisions based on fear. Make decisions based on hope and possibility."

Your educational journey does not have to be one of stress. It will become much easier for you once you have mastered effective study habits and the magic of time management.

## STRESS TO SUCCESS: MAKE SCHOOL WORK FOR YOU

Navigating the academic landscape can often feel like riding a high-stakes rollercoaster, and academic stress is the unexpected loop-the-loop that comes with the territory. According to Scott (2018):

> A little stress can be a great motivator, as any student can tell you. A lot of stress, however, can often create more of an obstacle than a benefit. This is true regarding many things, including health-promoting behaviors, relationships, and memories. Stress can inhibit the way we form and retrieve memories and can affect how our memory works. (para 1)

As Scott (2018, para 3) further explains, "Stress can affect how memories are formed. When stressed, people have a more difficult time creating short-term memories and turning those short-term memories into long-term memories, meaning that it is more difficult to learn."

These insights highlight the profound impact of academic stress on your cognitive function and memory recall. It's as if your brain's superhero powers fade when stress takes center stage. But don't worry; we've got you covered with strategies to manage stress like a pro. As per P. Reynolds (2022):

According to the American Psychological Association's Stress in America 2020 survey, teens who are already under stress due to the normal pressures of high school have felt even more stress in recent years, thanks to the pandemic. About 43 percent of teens surveyed in 2020 said their stress levels had increased, and 45 percent said they had difficulty concentrating on schoolwork. Many reported feeling less motivated. (para 2)

These statistics underline the real-world challenges students face, especially in the context of elevated stress levels. However, we're here to equip you with a toolbox of strategies not just to survive but to thrive in your academic pursuits. From deep breathing exercises to well-structured study schedules, we aim to help you harness your stress and turn it into a stepping stone toward academic success.

## MORE THAN SCRIBBLES: THE POWER OF NOTE-TAKING

In the exciting world of learning, taking great notes is one super skill that can make a massive difference. You are probably thinking, "Notes? Really?" Yes, really! According to Preston (2018):

Taking great notes is about helping you to get organized, stay focused, remember key points, and study effectively for tests. It's not about recording every word a teacher says or everything an expert writes. If you try that, you'll be more focused on taking notes than on understanding the material. (para 3)

Life can get pretty hectic with school, extracurricular activities, and other commitments. Notes are like your trusty sidekick, helping you keep everything in order. When you jot down the important stuff, it's like creating a roadmap to guide you through your learning journey. No more getting lost in the sea of information!

We've all been there—sitting in class or studying, and suddenly, your mind wanders. Taking notes is your secret weapon to stay engaged. It's like actively participating in the learning process. You are not just listening; you are interacting with the material. It's like saying to your brain, "Hey, pay attention, this is important!"

Have you ever felt like you studied for hours but still couldn't remember what you learned? Notes to the rescue! When you write down the essential stuff, your brain has an easier time locking it into memory. It's like boosting your memory so you can recall the important details when you need them.

Let's face it; there's a lot to learn. When tests roll around, your notes become your study buddies. They're like your cheat sheet to success. Well-organized notes allow you to review, revise, and prepare for tests more effectively. It's not about recording every word but capturing the most crucial ideas.

Here's the trick: Taking great notes isn't about writing down every word your teacher says or copying every word from your textbook. Preston (2018) wisely advises that it's not about being a human recording machine. Instead, it's about focusing on what matters most, on what helps you understand the material. It's about picking out the gems from the sea of words.

So, whether in class, at a workshop, or reading a fascinating book, remember that your notes are your secret weapon. They are your path to organization, focus, memory, and successful studying. It's time to unlock the power of note-taking and take control of your learning journey!

### Choose Your Note-Taking Method

### The Cornell Method

This method divides your paper into three sections: a narrow left column, a wider right column, and a section at the bottom. In the right column, you jot down your main notes during the lecture or reading. The left column is for cues or questions to help you review later, and the bottom section summarizes the main ideas after the lecture or reading.

### Outlining

Outlining might be your go-to method if you like structured, hierarchical thinking. You create a hierarchical structure for your notes, with main topics at the top and indented subtopics and details beneath them.

### Charting

This method works well when you need to compare and contrast different pieces of information. Create a table or chart, and use columns and rows to organize your notes.

*Handwritten vs. Digital Notes*

In the ever-evolving education landscape, note-taking methods have transformed over the years. Traditional pen and paper have faced competition from laptops, mobile devices, and software applications. This shift gained even more momentum with the onset of the COVID-19 pandemic in 2020, as schools worldwide transitioned to online learning. This digital note-taking approach became a lifeline for educators and students alike, and it appears it's here to stay. Research indicates online learning can improve information retention (Bouchrika, 2021).

However, the age-old debate of handwritten versus digital notes lingers. Studies suggest that handwritten notes promote better memory and understanding compared to typing. The physical act of writing engages the brain more deeply. But the choice between these methods is more than a one-size-fits-all answer (Effectiviology, 2019).

Opting for the traditional handwritten approach can be a potent tool to enhance your retention and comprehension. The tactile connection between pen and paper can be a game-changer for many students. Keep your handwritten notes well-organized in a notebook or folder to make the most of this method.

On the other hand, digital note-taking offers its own set of advantages. It's efficient, searchable, and eco-friendly. This approach is particularly suitable for those who prefer typing or need seamless access to their notes across various devices. Applications like OneNote, Evernote, or GoodNotes can be invaluable tools. However, exercise caution and resist the temptation to wander into the abyss of web surfing during your note-taking sessions.

## *Maximize Your Note-Taking Efficiency*

### Color-Coding

Use different colors for various categories or concepts. For instance, you might use blue for main ideas, green for examples, and red for definitions. This visual distinction can help you quickly spot and review key points.

### Shorthand

Develop a personal shorthand system to save time while jotting down notes. For example, use "&" for "and," "w/" for "with," or "->" for "leads to." Please make a list of your shorthand symbols and practice using them.

### Symbols

Employ symbols like arrows (for cause-and-effect relationships), asterisks (for important points), or exclamation marks (for something you don't understand and need to revisit).

By experimenting with these methods and techniques, you will soon discover the note-taking style that suits you best and helps you thrive in your studies. Remember, your notes are like treasure maps that guide you to academic success!

## YOUR PERFECT STUDY FORMULA

Your ideal study strategy should make learning more exciting and engaging. It's time to take an active role in your education instead of just sitting back and watching.

So, you know how sometimes school feels like watching a show, with lectures and textbooks? Well, this passive way of learning is less effective. It can leave you feeling like you are just an audience member in your education (Peer 2022). But guess what? You can change that!

Choosing the right study method is super important. Most students use strategies like re-reading their notes, which don't work that well. We're here to tell you that there's a much more awesome way to learn.

Active learning is like becoming the star of your learning show. It's not just about listening; it's about doing. It can involve discussions, hands-on projects, and applying what you have learned in real-life situations (Peer, 2022).

And don't worry; you can still use your textbooks and have some great classroom moments. Active learning can include traditional methods like lectures (Peer, 2022). But it takes things up a notch by actively involving you.

So, your perfect study formula is about becoming the hero of your learning journey. You get to be in charge, summarize in your own words, ask questions, and apply your knowledge to real-life situations. This way, you will not only understand better, but you will remember what you have learned for much longer.

## POPULAR STUDY METHODS

### The SQR3 Method (Survey, Question, Read, Recall, Review)

The SQR3 method is your roadmap to effective textbook reading. Start by surveying the text—quickly flip through the pages, checking headings, subheadings, and study aids like summaries or questions. This gives you an overview. Then, create questions that you aim to answer while reading. As you read, stay actively engaged by answering those questions. After finishing a section, take a moment to recall what you have learned. Finally, review your notes and highlighted sections to consolidate your understanding.

### Retrieval Practice

The power of retrieval practice lies in the effortful process of recalling information. Create flashcards with questions on one side and answers on the other, or challenge yourself with self-quizzes. This process strengthens the neural pathways associated with the material you are studying, enhancing your long-term memory.

### The Pomodoro Technique

Pomodoro is your time management ally. Allocate a specific task to a 25-minute "Pomodoro." After completing it, reward yourself with a 5-minute break. This cycle continues for four Pomodoros, after which you can take a longer break. This method boosts your concentration and productivity by breaking your study session into manageable chunks.

## The Feynman Technique

The Feynman Technique invites you to understand a topic deeply by teaching it to others or simplifying it as if you were teaching a child. This forces you to articulate the material in a way that demonstrates true comprehension. If you find it challenging to explain a complex concept in simple terms, it's an indicator that you need to revisit and clarify your understanding.

## Spaced Repetition

Spaced repetition is like a personalized memory booster. It schedules your study sessions to maximize recall efficiency. Review material more frequently initially and then at longer intervals. It's particularly effective for language learning, historical facts, or any subject requiring memorization.

## The PQ4R Method (Preview, Question, Read, Reflect, Recite, Review):

PQ4R builds on the basics of reading. Begin with a preview of the material. Formulate questions based on your understanding of the text, which you will aim to answer while reading. Actively engage with the content, reflecting on its significance. After each section, recite the key points from memory. Finally, review the entire material to connect the dots and ensure comprehension.

## Leitner System

The Leitner System uses a series of boxes to sort flashcards. Correct answers promote moving a card to a box with longer intervals before it's reviewed again, while incorrect answers bring a card back to a shorter interval. This efficient approach ensures that you spend more time reviewing difficult material, ultimately optimizing your retention.

## Color-Coded Notes

Color-coding can breathe life into your notes. Use different colors for headings, key points, definitions, and examples. Visual cues can make your notes more organized and memorable. For example, important formulas or dates might be highlighted in a bright, attention-grabbing color.

## Mind Mapping

Mind maps let you visualize complex topics. Start with a central idea and branch out to subtopics and supporting details. This visual representation helps you see connections, making it easier to grasp and remember information. It's especially effective for concepts that involve interconnected ideas.

You can discover your perfect study formula by experimenting with these study methods and strategies. Remember that active learning is often the key to understanding and retaining information, and creating an optimal study environment can work wonders for your academic journey.

## DISCIPLINE IS ACTUALLY COOL

Discipline is the secret sauce that helps you maintain focus and diligence in your academic journey. To harness this power, cultivate effective habits and routines. These habits can transform your academic life by structuring your day and helping you navigate the complexity of assignments and studying.

Creating habits and routines is like laying down the tracks for a well-functioning train. Once the tracks are in place, your journey becomes more predictable and your goals more attainable. Consider waking up at the same time each day, dedicating a specific time for study sessions, or committing to daily exercise. Routines eliminate the need for constant decision-making, which frees up mental space for more important tasks. These habits and routines are your companions on your journey to academic excellence.

### *Developing Good Study Habits*

Effective study habits are the cornerstone of academic success. The right habits can help you focus, stay organized, and maximize your study sessions.

Here are some tips to help you develop those habits:

- **Set a schedule:** Establish a consistent study schedule. This will help you get into the groove, as your brain will recognize it as study time.

- **Find a suitable environment**: Create a dedicated study space free from distractions. Ensure that it's comfortable, well-lit, and organized.
- **Use active learning:** Engage with the material actively by summarizing, teaching, or quizzing yourself. Active learning enhances retention.
- **Time management:** Manage your time effectively. The Pomodoro Technique, discussed earlier, can be a valuable tool for breaking your study time into manageable segments.
- **Take regular breaks:** Don't forget to include breaks in your study schedule. Short breaks boost concentration and prevent burnout.
- **Seek help when needed:** If you are struggling with a particular subject or concept, don't hesitate to seek help from your teachers or classmates.

### Procrastination: The Enemy of Discipline

Procrastination is a formidable adversary to your self-discipline. It's like a magnetic force that pulls you away from tasks that require focus and effort.

To combat procrastination, consider these strategies:

- **Set specific goals:** Clearly define your goals. This can make tasks less overwhelming and increase motivation.
- **Prioritize tasks:** Break your tasks into smaller, manageable steps and tackle them individually. You will

feel a sense of accomplishment as you complete each step.

- **Use time management techniques:** Time-blocking and to-do lists can help you allocate time to different tasks. Set deadlines and stick to them.
- **Identify your triggers:** Understand what causes your procrastination. Is it boredom, stress, or the task's complexity? Identifying triggers can help you address the root cause.
- **Minimize distractions:** Create a focused study environment by removing potential distractions like your phone, social media, or noisy surroundings.

Remember, discipline is not about depriving yourself of leisure or relaxation. It's about striking a balance between work and personal time. By embracing discipline and cultivating positive habits, you are taking the reins of your academic journey and setting yourself up for success.

## THE EXAM COUNTDOWN: CRUSH IT WITHOUT CRASHING

Creating a study timetable isn't just about jotting down hours on paper. It's a strategic approach to help you navigate your study materials effectively.

Start by listing all the subjects or topics you must cover for your exams. It's essential to understand which subjects require more attention than others. Be honest with yourself about your strengths and weaknesses in each area. For example, if you are a math whiz but struggle with history, allocate more time to history studies.

Break down your study sessions into manageable segments. For instance, divide it into specific time slots or chapters if you have a vast history curriculum. This approach helps prevent you from feeling overwhelmed and allows you to focus on a particular aspect of the subject at a time.

Design a visual study calendar that offers a clear overview of your study plan. This calendar can be a physical one hanging on your wall, a digital tool, or an app designed for academic planning. Make sure to mark important dates, such as exam days, assignment deadlines, and review sessions. A visual aid like this can make tracking your progress and staying organized easier.

Avoid the pitfall of cramming, which can be counterproductive. Instead, distribute your study time evenly across different subjects and topics. One effective technique to consider is the Pomodoro Technique. As we discussed before, this method involves breaking your study time into focused intervals—for example, a good session length is typically 25 minutes—followed by short breaks. After a few cycles, you can take a more extended break to give your brain a chance to process the information you are consuming. This balanced approach ensures you maintain productivity while preventing burnout. You can, of course, tweak the time this process takes as you learn what works best for your learning habits.

## *The Role of Mock Tests and Past Papers*

Imagine mock tests and past exam papers as your secret weapons for acing exams with style! These study buddies are like your trusty sidekicks, guiding you through the adventure of exam preparation and helping you shine in the spotlight of success.

Mock tests can be your practice runs for the real deal. Picture them as your own personal dress rehearsal, letting you experience the excitement and challenges of the actual exam. Why is this so cool? Well, it's like getting the inside scoop on the format and timing of the exam, so when the big day arrives, you are ready to tackle each question like a superhero. Time management skills? Nailed it!

Past exam papers give you a sneak peek into the questions you might face and how detailed your answers should be. It's like having a treasure map that helps you uncover patterns, key concepts, and areas where you might want to do a bit more exploring.

But here's the best part—practicing with these past papers isn't just about studying; it's your secret sauce for identifying what you already rock at and where you could use a little more superhero training. Think of it as your personalized guide, showing you the way to becoming a true exam superhero!

### Exam Preparation Tips

As you prepare for exams, consider summarizing your notes to capture key points succinctly. This practice enables you to review more efficiently and reinforces your understanding of the material.

Teaching what you have learned to someone else is a powerful method for consolidating your knowledge. Explain complex concepts to a friend, family member, or even an imaginary student, and use this process to reinforce your understanding.

Mnemonic devices are memory aids, such as acronyms or rhymes, that help you remember complex information. Utilize these strategies to remember key points and formulas.

Regularly reviewing and revising your notes is crucial. Schedule time for quick daily or weekly reviews to refresh your memory and maintain the material in your long-term memory.

### Easing Exam Anxiety with Relaxation Techniques

Stress and anxiety often accompany exam preparations, but finding ways to relax and manage these emotions is vital.

Deep, slow breaths can calm your mind and reduce anxiety. Practice deep breathing exercises regularly, especially when you feel overwhelmed or stressed. One effective technique is to inhale deeply for a count of four, hold for four, exhale for four, and pause for four before repeating.

Progressive muscle relaxation involves tensing and then relaxing different muscle groups. This technique is an excellent way to release physical tension. Begin by tensing a specific muscle group for several seconds and then relax it completely. Continue this process throughout your body, working from your toes to your head.

Meditation can help you focus your mind and relieve stress. You don't need to be an expert meditator to benefit from this practice. Many guided meditation apps and videos are available for free, which can lead you through mindfulness exercises and meditation sessions.

### The Importance of Sleep

In the critical days of your exams, establishing a solid foundation for success involves more than just hitting the books. Prioritizing a good night's sleep is a game-changer for optimal cognitive function. A well-rested mind doesn't just show up—it shines, excelling in memory retention, focus, and problem-solving prowess. So, commit to getting seven to nine hours of quality sleep each night—an investment that pays off in As.

To enhance your sleep quality, consider incorporating the following practices into your routine:

- **Maintain a consistent sleep schedule:** Treat your sleep like a VIP by sticking to a regular bedtime and wake-up time, even on weekends. This consistent routine syncs up with your body's internal clock, ensuring you are in peak condition when it's time to perform.

- **Create a relaxing bedtime routine:** Transform your pre-sleep rituals into a sanctuary of calm. Enjoy soothing activities like reading, gentle stretches, or a warm bath. These calming moments signal to your brain that it's time to wind down and prepare for a rejuvenating night's rest.
- **Limit screen time:** The glow of screens might be tempting, but the blue light they emit can throw a wrench into your sleep plans. Dodge the disruption by steering clear of screens at least an hour before bedtime. Your sleep will thank you, and so will your exam scores.
- **Watch your diet:** Fuel your body with the right ingredients for a restful night. Avoid heavy meals and caffeine close to bedtime, as they disrupt sleep. Opt for light, sleep-friendly snacks if hunger strikes late at night. Your body will appreciate the nourishment without the nighttime interference.

By seamlessly integrating these elements into your exam preparation routine, you are not just studying—you are crafting a holistic strategy for success. Your study timetable becomes a well-oiled machine, preparatory materials are absorbed with heightened efficiency, relaxation techniques become second nature, and your well-rested self is primed to tackle the challenges of exam day. With unwavering dedication and a meticulously structured plan, you are not just on the path to success— you are destined to ace those exams! Sweet dreams and even sweeter results await.

## ACTIVITY: TIME-TAMING: CRAFTING YOUR STUDY SCHEDULE

Preparing an effective study schedule is crucial for academic success. Let's embark on a journey to create your personalized study schedule. Follow these steps to allocate time wisely and maintain a healthy balance between study and relaxation.

**Step 1: Set Clear Goals**

Before crafting your schedule, you must identify your academic goals and what you want to achieve with your studies. Understand the subjects, topics, and tasks that require your focus.

**Step 2: Assess Your Commitments**

Consider your daily and weekly commitments. Consider class timings, extracurricular activities, part-time jobs, and other responsibilities. This step ensures that your schedule aligns with your life outside of academics.

**Step 3: Time Blocking**

It's time to create a visual representation of your daily schedule. Divide your day into blocks of time, typically from when you wake up to when you go to bed. Allocate time for your commitments, including classes, meals, and personal routines.

**Step 4: Prioritize Your Subjects and Topics**

Identify your most challenging subjects or topics; these should be given prime slots when you are most alert and focused. Place them during your "peak hours" to optimize your learning experience—reserve easier or less demanding tasks when your energy might be lower.

**Step 5: Buffer Time and Planned Breaks**

One common mistake in scheduling is not accounting for buffer time and planned breaks. It's essential to include short breaks between study sessions to recharge. These breaks might be 5–10 minutes, during which you can stretch, grab a snack, or do a quick relaxation exercise.

At the end of each focused study block, allocate a longer break (15–30 minutes). This is your time to unwind, move around, or practice relaxation techniques. These planned breaks are crucial for maintaining productivity and preventing burnout.

**Step 6: Weekly and Monthly Planning**

To ensure your schedule remains organized and flexible, it's helpful to create both weekly and monthly overviews:

- **Weekly planning:** At the beginning of each week, assess your assignments, upcoming quizzes or tests, and any projects. Allocate time slots for each task throughout the week. This way, you can spread your workload evenly and avoid last-minute cramming.
- **Monthly planning:** On a broader scale, you can create a monthly calendar or use digital tools to note important dates, such as exams, assignment deadlines, or extracurricular events. This monthly overview helps you maintain a long-term perspective on your academic commitments.

**Step 7: Regular Review and Adaptation**

Regularly review your schedule and adjust it as necessary. Life can be unpredictable, and your study needs may change. Adapt to unforeseen circumstances and refine your schedule to maximize productivity and maintain balance.

**Step 8: Staying Accountable**

Consider sharing it with a friend or family member to hold yourself accountable to your schedule. They can help remind you of your commitments and provide moral support.

Remember, your study schedule should be a dynamic tool that evolves as your needs change. Be kind to yourself and allow room for flexibility. With a consistent commitment to your schedule and regular review, you will find that crafting an efficient study schedule is an invaluable skill for academic success. Happy scheduling!

## AFFIRMATIONS: VIRTUAL STUDY BUDDIES AND MINDSET MANTRAS

Staying on top of your studies requires the right mindset and tools. In this section, you will discover a treasure trove of websites and apps designed to make your academic journey more manageable.

*Websites and Apps for Effective Studying*

- **Quizlet:** Create custom flashcards, practice quizzes, and interactive study games. It's a fun way to learn and test your knowledge.
- **Khan Academy:** Offers comprehensive video lessons and practice exercises covering various subjects. It's a fantastic resource for students of all ages.
- **Coursera:** Access courses from top universities and institutions worldwide. Learn at your own pace with video lectures and quizzes.
- **Duolingo:** If you are learning a new language, Duolingo offers an engaging way to practice vocabulary and grammar.
- **Evernote:** A powerful note-taking app that lets you organize your thoughts, lectures, and research in one place.
- **Grammarly:** Improve your writing with real-time grammar and spell-check, as well as suggestions for enhancing your writing style.
- **Forest**: A unique app that encourages productivity by growing a virtual tree while you study. If you leave the app, your tree dies, which can be a great motivator to stay focused.
- **Google Scholar**: Access a vast collection of scholarly articles and academic papers for your research needs.
- **Trello:** A fantastic project management tool that helps you stay organized. Create boards for your classes, to-do lists, and important dates.

- **LibriVox**: For literature lovers, LibriVox provides free audiobooks of classic literature. It's a great way to make your reading assignments more engaging.

### Mindset Mantras for Academic Success

In addition to using these tools, cultivating a positive and disciplined mindset is essential for academic achievement. Affirmations can be your secret weapon for staying motivated and focused.

Repeat these affirmations regularly to boost your confidence and determination:

- "I am capable of learning anything I set my mind to."
- "I embrace challenges as opportunities for growth."
- "My focus and dedication will lead me to success."
- "I am in control of my time and use it wisely."
- "Each study session brings me one step closer to my goals."
- "I believe in my ability to excel academically."
- "I am resilient and can overcome any obstacle in my path."
- "Success is the result of my consistent efforts."
- "I trust in my capacity to learn and achieve my dreams."
- "I approach my studies with curiosity and enthusiasm."

Remember, you are not alone on this academic journey. With the right resources and a positive mindset, you can tackle any subject or challenge that comes your way. Keep these websites, apps, and affirmations close to inspire and support your academic endeavors.

---

# 6

# IT'S OKAY NOT TO BE OKAY

In the words of Demi Lovato, "Go on and try to tear me down; I will be rising from the ground." Just like a skyscraper, we all have the strength to rise, no matter how tough the challenges we face.

Adolescence can be an emotional rollercoaster, and it's completely normal to experience highs and lows. But what sets you apart is your ability to understand and manage these emotions.

Your emotions are what makes you wonderfully human.

## THE FEELS A-Z: UNDERSTANDING YOUR EMOTIONS

Emotions are like the colors of a vibrant painting, each hue painting a unique story. "The concept of emotion may seem simple, but scientists often have trouble agreeing on what it means. Most scientists believe that emotions involve things other than just feelings" (Cowen 2018, para 2). From the joyful strokes of laughter to the somber shades of tears, emotions are the brushstrokes that color our lives during the incredible journey of adolescence. "They involve bodily reactions, like when your heart races because you feel excited. They also involve expressive movements, including facial expressions and sounds" (Cowen 2018, para 2).

Cowen (2018) further notes, "Although there are many different parts of an emotion, feelings are usually considered the most important. The majority of scientists who study emotion measure it by asking people what they are feeling" (para 3). Of course, self-reported experiences have their limitations, but, as Cowen adds, "self-reported experience, meaning what a person says about what he or she is feeling, is the most direct way to measure emotional feelings" (para 3). Think of feelings as the vibrant colors that dominate the canvas of emotions, serving as the palette from which the artist chooses to express their emotional landscape.

The emotional world is vast, from happiness to sadness, excitement to fear, and everything in between. It's this incredible diversity of feelings that makes us beautifully human. As Felton (2022) puts it, "Emotion is typically defined as a complicated response to certain situations, often involving behavioral, experiential, and physiological factors" (para 4). Emotions, as Felton continues, "are how you deal with circumstances that are personally important" (para 4). They are the vivid strokes that shape the narrative of our lives, revealing how we cope with personally significant circumstances.

Emotional literacy is a crucial skill. It involves understanding one's emotions and feelings and effectively communicating one's emotional patterns. Like learning a new language, emotional literacy allows you to comprehend and express your feelings better, fostering deeper connections with others. "Emotional Literacy is the ability to understand your emotions, the ability to listen to others and empathize with their emotions, and the ability to express emotions productively" (GIETU, 2022, para 4).

### *Emotions Broke Down*

### ✚ Positive Emotions

Positive emotions are like the sunshine of our hearts, casting warmth and brightening our smiles. They infuse our lives with vibrancy and turn each day into a new adventure. As you navigate the exciting world of adolescence, you will encounter a colorful array of positive emotions, each with its own unique charm.

Here are some examples of the positive emotions that can light up your world:

- **Joy:** Imagine the feeling of bubbling happiness that springs from within. It can come from reaching a personal goal, receiving fantastic news, or simply spending time with cherished friends.
- **Happiness:** It's that sense of contentment and well-being that washes over you. You experience it when you

are doing something you love or sharing laughter with friends.

- **Excitement:** Excitement is like a spark that ignites your enthusiasm. It's the anticipation of upcoming events, whether it's a party, a trip, or the release of a new book.
- **Love:** Love is a profound and powerful emotion. It can be the romantic love for a partner, the love of family and friends, or the affection you feel for a beloved pet.
- **Contentment:** Contentment is the peaceful feeling of being in harmony with yourself and your surroundings. It envelops you when you are engrossed in a good book or strolling in nature.
- **Amusement:** It's the delightful laughter that escapes when you find something funny. A joke, a funny movie, or your friends' humorous antics can trigger it.
- **Elation:** Elation is an intense form of happiness, often experienced during significant life events like acing a test, fulfilling a dream, or celebrating a milestone.
- **Satisfaction:** Satisfaction is that rewarding feeling of accomplishment after a job well done, whether it's completing a challenging project or excelling in a hobby.
- **Hope:** Hope is a positive outlook on the future, the belief that things will improve and that you can conquer challenges.

These positive emotions are like the vibrant colors in the palette of your life's painting. They light up your world and remind you that each day holds the potential for happiness and fulfillment. Embrace them, cherish them, and draw strength from them in both everyday moments and extraordinary ones.

## — Negative Emotions

On the other side of the emotional spectrum, we encounter a range of negative emotions. These feelings, such as sadness, anger, fear, and disgust, can often be challenging and uncomfortable. But it's crucial to understand that they play a vital role in our lives.

Let's delve into these emotions and discover why they are essential for our well-being:

- **Sadness:** Sadness is a deep emotion that often arises in response to loss, disappointment, or unmet expectations. While it can be uncomfortable, sadness helps us process and heal from challenging experiences. It encourages seeking support from others and reflecting on what truly matters to us.
- **Anger:** Anger is a natural response to situations we perceive as unjust, frustrating, or threatening. This emotion can motivate us to take action and assert our boundaries. When managed constructively, anger can lead to positive changes and conflict resolution.
- **Fear:** Fear is a primal emotion designed to keep us safe. It emerges when we encounter potential threats, whether physical or emotional. Fear triggers a "fight or flight" response, helping us react quickly to danger. It's an essential survival mechanism.

- **Disgust:** Disgust is our response to things that are unclean, offensive, or harmful. It helps us avoid harmful substances or situations, contributing to our physical well-being.

While negative emotions may feel challenging, they are crucial for our emotional and physical well-being. They serve as valuable signals, alerting us to potential threats, helping us process difficult experiences, and motivating us to take action. Acknowledging and understanding these emotions is important, as they can offer valuable insights into our inner world and guide our responses to various life situations. Embracing these emotions as a natural part of the human experience can lead to personal growth and resilience. Remember, it's okay to feel these emotions, and they can lead to positive outcomes when managed in a healthy and constructive way.

**Complex Emotions**

Our emotional world resembles a beautifully woven tapestry filled with intricate colors and patterns. Sometimes, we experience emotions that are a blend of both positive and negative feelings, creating a unique and complex emotional landscape. These emotions may seem like a mix of contradictions, but they add depth and richness to our lives.

Let's explore a few complex emotions and why they're essential:

- **Grief:** Grief is a complex emotion that arises when we experience loss, like when a loved one passes away or an important chapter of our lives ends. It often brings feelings of sadness and sorrow. But here's the remarkable thing about grief—it also reflects the deep love and connection we share with what or who we've lost. So, even though it feels heavy, it reminds us of the beautiful bonds we've had.

- **Nostalgia**: Nostalgia is like a bittersweet melody that plays in our hearts. It's a mix of happiness and a touch of sadness. When you feel nostalgic, you are remembering the good times of the past—the fun vacations, the inside jokes, and the people who shaped your life. This emotion may bring a smile to your face, but it can also tug at your heart because those moments can't be relived.
- **Bittersweet feelings:** Imagine the feeling of your heart dancing to a melody with both upbeat and mellow notes. That's what bittersweet emotions are like— they're a fusion of happiness and sadness. You might experience them when you graduate from school or say goodbye to a place you have loved. They show that life is a beautiful blend of new beginnings and memories that stay in your heart.

These complex emotions are like the secret colors on your canvas, making your life's painting more vibrant and meaningful. They remind us that it's perfectly normal to feel a mix of emotions at the same time. Embracing these feelings helps us connect with our inner selves and fully appreciate the rich tapestry of our lives. So, the next time you experience a bittersweet moment, know that you are living life to the fullest, savoring the beauty in moments that are both bitter and sweet and sometimes, everything in between.

## Mood States

Mood states are like the ever-changing landscapes of our emotional world. Unlike specific emotions that can come and go in a flash, moods are the background colors on the canvas of our lives, painting a more persistent and long-lasting emotional picture. These emotional backdrops can span a vast spectrum, much like the seasons and weather patterns that bring variety to our days.

Mood states can linger for hours, days, or even longer, affecting how you perceive and interact with the world. They're not only influenced by external events but can also be shaped by your thoughts and internal experiences. Acknowledging and understanding your mood states can provide insights into your emotional well-being and help you navigate the ever-shifting emotional landscapes that make life such a rich and diverse journey. So, whether your mood is radiant like a sunny day or reflective like a soft, rainy evening, embrace it as an integral part of your unique emotional world.

## Social Emotions

Imagine emotions as the colorful threads that weave the intricate tapestry of your social life. Amid the tapestry of human interactions, you will find social emotions, each thread representing a unique feeling that connects us to others.

- **Empathy:** When a friend shares their joys or sorrows, you don't just listen; you step into their emotional shoes. Empathy is the ability to understand and share the feelings of another, creating a bridge of understanding between people. It's like lending someone your emotional umbrella when it rains in their world.

- **Guilt:** Guilt is the gentle nudge of conscience, reminding you when you have strayed from your values or hurt someone unintentionally. It's like an inner compass guiding you back onto the path of empathy and kindness.

- **Shame:** While guilt helps us realign with our values, shame often leads to self-reflection. It's like a mirror that encourages us to examine our actions, guiding us to become better versions of ourselves.

- **Pride:** Pride isn't just about boasting; it's about recognizing and celebrating your achievements. Like a badge of honor, it stands as a testament to your hard work and dedication.

- **Gratitude:** Gratitude is the warm embrace of appreciation. It reminds us to acknowledge the kindness of others and the gifts life bestows upon us. It's like a bouquet of thank-you flowers to those who enrich our lives.

These social emotions play a critical role in the complex web of human relationships. They help us understand, support, and connect with one another, enhancing our social bonds and strengthening the threads of empathy, compassion, and trust.

122 | MAUREEN GIANNOTTI

So, as you navigate the labyrinth of human connections, remember that these social emotions are your emotional compass, guiding you toward richer, more meaningful relationships

As an adolescent, you are in a unique phase of life where emotions can be especially intense and sometimes bewildering. Your emotional journey may often resemble a rollercoaster, but remember that these feelings are perfectly normal and an integral part of growing up.

Understanding emotions is like mastering a complex language —one that has no grammar or vocabulary but is universal to all humans. Emotions are your guides, helping you decipher your inner world and connect with others. In the chapters that follow, we'll delve into this emotional realm, offering insights and techniques to help you embrace your feelings and harness their power for a more fulfilling and authentic life.

## EMOTIONAL TRIGGERS: THE BOOBY TRAPS OF YOUR MIND

Imagine these triggers as hidden surprises or traps on your emotional journey, and let's unravel their secrets together.

Emotional triggers are like those secret switches in your heart that can unleash powerful emotions. They're like the tripwires of your mind, connected to a vault of feelings waiting to burst out. When one of these triggers is activated, it's like a burst of emotion taking over your thoughts, feelings, and actions. Sometimes, it's a happy burst, like when you see a photo of your childhood best friend, and you are flooded with nostalgia. But other times, it's not so pleasant—like when someone comments on your appearance, and it stirs up insecurities.

These emotional triggers have a special connection to your past experiences. Some triggers can bring up wonderful memories, while others might stir up distress. Think of it this way: your mind is like a treasure chest filled with memories, and these triggers are like keys that unlock certain emotions. For example, imagine a memory of a fun day at the amusement park with friends—that's a positive trigger. It can make you feel joyful, happy, and excited.

But there's another side, too. Suppose someone mentions something that reminds you of a not-so-great time, like a difficult moment in the past or an unkind comment. That can activate a different kind of trigger, one that may bring up sadness, anger, or frustration.

Now, while emotional triggers can be a bit like rollercoasters for your feelings, remember, it's all part of being beautifully human. Understanding your triggers can help you navigate the ups and downs of your emotions and even improve your relationships with others. So, embrace your emotional journey, and let's keep exploring this incredible world together!

### Why Are Emotional Triggers So Potent?

Emotional triggers are compelling because they operate on a subconscious level. They don't knock on your mind's door, seeking permission to enter; they burst right in, dictating your emotional responses. It's like a reflex, fast and unthinking. The strength of this reaction can sometimes catch you off guard.

In real-life scenarios, emotional triggers may appear as subtle as the trigger of a camera, snapping your emotions into focus.

Here are a few everyday examples:

- **Conflict aversion:** If you had a traumatic argument in your past, any confrontation, even a minor one, can trigger a strong emotional reaction, causing you to avoid disagreements at all costs.
- **Neglect:** A history of feeling overlooked can make you hypersensitive to neglect. Even a brief perceived slight can send your emotions spiraling.
- **Abandonment:** If you have experienced abandonment in your life, you might react strongly to even temporary separations, such as when a close friend can't meet up with you due to other commitments.
- **Disapproval:** If you grew up with strict expectations, the fear of disapproval may have become an emotional trigger. It can make you excessively anxious about making mistakes or receiving criticism.

### Identifying Your Emotional Triggers

Discovering your emotional triggers is like exploring a hidden treasure map within your mind. You may easily recognize some, especially if they've been causing turbulence in your life, while others may lurk in the shadows, awaiting discovery.

Recording your experiences in a journal can be an excellent tool to help unearth your emotional triggers. When you experience a sudden, intense emotional reaction, take note of the situation, your feelings, and your immediate thoughts. After some reflection, you may start to notice recurring patterns. Identifying the source of these triggers is an essential first step toward reclaiming control over your emotional responses.

As you become more aware of your emotional triggers, you will gain a deeper understanding of the underlying beliefs or memories that drive them. Armed with this self-awareness, you can begin the journey of neutralizing their power and shaping more balanced and intentional emotional responses in your daily life.

## BUILDING EMOTIONAL RESILIENCE: YOUR INNER SHOCK ABSORBER

Emotional resilience, girls, is your remarkable superpower, your inner shock absorber that helps you bounce back from the unexpected jolts and bumps that life throws. Just like a tough, all-terrain vehicle can navigate the roughest roads, emotional resilience equips you to handle the rollercoaster ride of life.

Picture emotional resilience as a toolbox filled with mental and emotional tools to help you navigate challenges, setbacks, and uncertainties. It's like having a trusty set of tools ready for anything that comes your way. Developing emotional resilience doesn't mean you won't face difficulties; you will meet them with more courage, strength, and adaptability.

Now, Roy Chowdhury (2019) describes emotional resilience as the ability to calm your mind after experiencing something negative. It's like having an inner drive that keeps you steady during life's downsides. Think of it as your very own inner superhero that guides you through the tough times.

This incredible inner strength plays a pivotal role in your emotional well-being. When you have emotional resilience, you are better equipped to manage stress, control your emotions, and keep a positive outlook even in challenging situations. But it doesn't stop there. Your emotional resilience has a ripple effect, influencing your academic performance, relationships with friends and family, and personal growth.

So, remember, you have got this incredible superpower within you. It's your emotional resilience, and it's there to help you not just survive life's ups and downs but to thrive and become the amazing person you are meant to be. Keep embracing your emotional journey, and let your resilience shine through!

**Practical Tips for Building Emotional Resilience**

Coping skills are like the tools in your emotional resilience toolbox. They help you manage stress and face adversity. Skills like deep breathing, mindfulness, and problem-solving can enhance your ability to bounce back from difficult experiences.

Your perspective shapes your reality. Learning to reframe challenges means viewing difficulties as opportunities for growth rather than insurmountable obstacles. For instance, a low grade on a test can be reframed as a chance to improve your study habits and academic performance.

Social support is a significant contributor to emotional resilience. Your friends and family can provide comfort, advice, and a listening ear during tough times. Remember, asking for help isn't a sign of weakness but a testament to your emotional strength.

Be as kind to yourself as you are to your best friend. Self-compassion involves treating yourself with the same care and empathy you would extend to others. When you make a mistake or face a setback, practicing self-compassion helps you bounce back with grace and self-love.

Unrealistic expectations can lead to disappointment and decreased resilience. Setting attainable goals and celebrating your progress along the way can keep you motivated and better equipped to face challenges.

### The Ripple Effect of Emotional Resilience

Emotional resilience isn't confined to your emotional well-being; it has a far-reaching ripple effect in your life. When you are emotionally resilient, you are better prepared to handle academic pressures. You can face challenging assignments, exams, and academic setbacks with poise and determination. Additionally, emotional resilience enhances your interpersonal skills, helping you build healthier and more meaningful relationships.

Cultivating emotional resilience is a lifelong journey, and you will continue to develop and strengthen it as you grow. The skills you learn now will serve as lifelong companions, empowering you to conquer challenges with grace and bounce back from life's hurdles with newfound strength.

## THE UNWANTED ROOMMATE AND HOW TO EVICT IT

Stress, my friends, can be a bit like an uninvited roommate crashing on your couch, showing up at the most inconvenient times, and making your life more challenging. It's that uninvited guest who tends to overstay their welcome, often making things more complicated than they need to be. And just like any unwanted guest, stress can take a toll on your body and mind, leaving you feeling less than your best.

Physiologically, as Chung (2022) notes, stress can lead to a range of symptoms like headaches, muscle tension, fatigue, and even digestive problems. It's as if your body is trying to send you signals, saying, "Hey, something's not quite right." Psychologically, stress can play tricks on your mind, leading to mood swings, anxiety, and sometimes even that feeling of being stuck in a never-ending tunnel of gloom, which we call depression.

But here's the interesting part: not all stress is bad. There's a kind of stress called eustress, or positive stress, which can be surprisingly motivating. It's like the nudge you need to study for that big exam, meet a deadline, or get ready for a sports competition. Eustress can be the kind of stress that encourages you to embrace challenges, filling you with motivation and enthusiasm for making positive changes in your life.

However, when stress takes on a darker form, it becomes distress, and that's the kind of stress that can truly feel over-whelming, like an uninvited guest who's taken over your whole house. Distress, as Chung (2022) describes, can leave you feeling debilitated, anxious, and unable to focus. It's the type of stress that can make everyday tasks seem like monumental challenges.

So, understanding stress is crucial, my friends. It's like knowing how to distinguish between that roommate who helps you grow and the one who overstays their welcome. Let's keep exploring this emotional journey and find ways to cope with the ups and downs of stress together!

### Stress Management Techniques

The good news is that, like any unwelcome roommate, stress can be managed and shown the door. We have a toolbox of stress management techniques to help you do just that.

Mindfulness practices can help you stay present, calm your racing thoughts, and reduce the impact of stress on your body and mind. Techniques like deep breathing, meditation, and progressive muscle relaxation are valuable tools.

Effective time management is like a shield against stress. When you have a well-organized schedule, you can minimize last-minute rushes and the stress they bring.

Simple habits like regular exercise, a balanced diet, and quality sleep can significantly reduce the impact of stress. When your body is well-nourished, it can better cope with the challenges that come your way.

Don't hesitate to reach out for help. Talking to friends, family, or a mental health professional can be an essential part of stress management. They can provide support, advice, and a listening ear when you need it most.

Create a personalized stress management plan that incorporates activities and practices that help you relieve stress and promote well-being. A well-thought-out plan can be a reliable guide in times of stress.

## ACTIVITY: SOULFUL BREATHING

Sometimes, all you need to manage stress and intense emotions is a few moments of mindful breathing and grounding techniques. Here, we'll guide you through some exercises that can be your secret tools in times of emotional turbulence.

**Mindful Breathing**

- Find a quiet, comfortable space where you can sit or lie down.
- Close your eyes if you feel comfortable doing so.
- Take a deep breath in through your nose, counting to four as you inhale.
- Hold your breath for a count of four.
- Exhale slowly through your mouth for a count of six.
- Repeat this process several times, letting each breath bring a sense of calm and relaxation.

**Box Breathing**

- Sit in a comfortable position and close your eyes.
- Inhale deeply through your nose while counting to four.
- Hold your breath for a count of four.
- Exhale through your mouth for a count of four.
- Pause and hold your breath for another count of four.
- Repeat this cycle for several minutes.

*Grounding Techniques*

**The 5-4-3-2-1 Technique**

1. Identify and name five things you can see around you.
2. Acknowledge four things you can touch or feel.
3. Recognize three things you can hear.
4. Notice two things you can smell.
5. Acknowledge one thing you can taste.

**Grounding through Body Scan**

1. Start by paying attention to your toes.
2. Gradually move your focus up your body, noting any sensations, tension areas, or relaxed areas.
3. This practice helps you reconnect with your physical self and become aware of bodily sensations.

## Counting

1. Counting is a simple grounding technique. Count from one to ten, or vice versa, several times.
2. You can also count your breaths, which enhances mindfulness.

## AFFIRMATIONS AND JOURNAL PROMPTS: THE EMOTIONAL PEP TALK

Emotions are like the weather; they come and go. To help you navigate the stormy days and celebrate the sunny ones, here's a list of emotionally uplifting affirmations to remind you of your inner strength.

### *Affirmations*

- "I acknowledge my emotions, and I am in control of how I respond to them."
- "I embrace my feelings, for they are a testament to my humanity."
- "I am resilient, and I can weather any emotional storm that comes my way."
- "I choose to let go of negative emotions and invite positivity into my life."
- "My emotions are valid, and I honor them without judgment."
- "I am learning and growing through every emotional experience."

- "I have the strength to turn my pain into power and my fear into curiosity."
- "I am not defined by my emotions; I am defined by my strength in facing them."

## *Journal Prompts*

- Reflect on a time when you felt overwhelmed by emotions. What was the situation, and what emotions were you experiencing?
- How did you cope with the situation mentioned in the previous prompt? Did your coping mechanism help you, or would you choose a different approach now?
- Describe a situation where you felt truly joyful and content. What caused these positive emotions, and how did you react to them?
- Think about a time when you felt anger. What were the circumstances, and how did you express your anger? How could you have handled it differently?
- What strategies or activities help you calm down when you are upset or agitated? How can you incorporate these techniques into your daily routine?
- Consider a place where you feel the safest and most comfortable. Describe it in detail and explain why it makes you feel secure.
- Write about a time when you felt sad or down. What contributed to those feelings? How did you ultimately overcome your sadness or regain your emotional balance?

# 7

# UNLOCK SECRETS TO HEALTHY RELATIONSHIPS

From family and friends to romantic partners, connections with others shape our experiences. But let's face it: not all relationships are created equal. Some lift us, bring out the best in us, and make us feel amazing. Others, however, can bring us down, make us question ourselves, and leave us feeling pretty yucky.

Eleanor Roosevelt (n.d.), a wise woman, once said, "No one can make you feel inferior without your consent." She meant that we can choose the relationships we're in and how those relationships make us feel. You will soon figure out which connections make you feel happy, supported, and like the amazing person you are, which might drag you down.

Just as you choose to eat healthy foods to nourish your body, it's just as important to choose relationships that positively feed your heart and mind.

## WHAT MAKES RELATIONSHIPS TICK?

In the exciting journey of growing up, relationships play a significant role. As young girls and teenagers, understanding the essence of relationships can profoundly impact our well-being and personal growth. The Office of Population Affairs (2022) notes, "Adolescents often try on different identities and roles, and all of these relationships contribute to their identity formation. Peers play a particularly big role in creating an identity during adolescence" (para 3).

Healthy relationships are like the strong foundation of a house. As the Office of Population Affairs (2022) suggests, trust is a cornerstone of any strong connection. Trust is believing you can rely on someone, confide in them, and know they have your back. The feeling of safety allows you to be your true self without fear. Trust is like the strong foundation that holds up a house, without which the relationship can crumble.

Communication is the bridge that connects our hearts and minds in any relationship. "Mutual trust, honesty, good communication, being understanding and calm during arguments, and consent" are the building blocks of healthy relationships, as emphasized by the Office of Population Affairs (2022). Open and honest communication is key. When we speak our minds and truly listen, we can resolve conflicts, learn from one another, and grow together. It's like the threads that weave our connections, making them stronger and more resilient.

Mutual respect is the pillar of a healthy relationship. It means valuing and treating each person with dignity. Everyone deserves to be treated with kindness and consideration in friendships, families, and romantic connections. Mutual respect creates a safe and caring space where you can be yourself without judgment. It's the glue that holds the relationship together.

As human beings, we are naturally inclined to seek out relationships. As the Office of Population Affairs (2022) suggests, adolescence is a period of rapid change, and relationships with friends play an important role as we become increasingly independent and develop our identities. These connections provide emotional support, opportunities for personal growth, and a sense of belonging. Just as we need food to nourish our bodies, we need relationships to feed our hearts and minds. Healthy relationships bring out the best in us, allowing us to grow, thrive, and flourish.

So, as you navigate adolescence's exciting and sometimes challenging path, remember the importance of healthy relationships. Cultivate trust, practice open communication, and always show mutual respect. These qualities will empower you to build strong and supportive connections that will enhance your journey of self-discovery and personal growth. In the intricate tapestry of life, these relationships are the vibrant threads that make it beautiful and fulfilling.

## THE GOOD, THE BAD, AND THE TOXIC: IDENTIFYING RELATIONSHIP TYPES

Navigating the relationship world can be like exploring a candy store with various sweet treats. Some relationships feel as delightful as your favorite candy, while others can leave a not-so-great taste in your mouth. We, as young girls and teenagers, must understand what makes these connections healthy, unhealthy, or even toxic.

Picture a beautiful garden filled with vibrant flowers, and think of healthy relationships as the blooming flowers. As Smith (2023) describes, these relationships thrive on trust, respect, open communication, and unwavering support. They provide a safe space where both partners contribute positively, much like the colors of a flourishing garden. Healthy relationships are a source of joy and fulfillment.

Imagine that same garden, but weeds and thorny vines overrun it. Unhealthy relationships might have their moments, but they also come with negativity. These connections can involve disrespect, poor communication, and an unequal balance of power, making you feel drained, unsupported, and anxious. Identifying these traits is essential because they can impact your well-being over time.

Toxic relationships can be likened to navigating a stormy sea with rough waters. As Rahman (2022) points out, they involve manipulation, disrespect, abuse, and a lack of support. These relationships can be emotionally and sometimes even physically harmful. It's crucial to recognize the signs of toxic relationships, as they can have lasting effects on your well-being.

Understanding where your relationship falls on this spectrum is just the first step. Once you have identified it, the next challenge is to figure out how to move forward. Transitioning from an unhealthy or toxic relationship to a healthy one is a journey that requires careful thought and courage. Your journey through the world of relationships is unique to you, and having this knowledge empowers you to make choices that lead to personal growth and well-being.

## SETTING BOUNDARIES: IT'S NOT RUDE, IT'S SMART

Boundaries in relationships are like personal safety zones that help define the limits of what you are comfortable with in various types of connections. These boundaries come in different forms, each crucial in maintaining healthy and fulfilling relationships.

Your emotional boundaries are like the compass guiding you through your feelings. They involve recognizing your emotions and understanding where you stand emotionally in your interactions with others. For instance, if someone repeatedly invalidates your feelings or disregards your emotions, it can be a sign of emotional boundary violation. It's important to express your feelings openly and honestly, as Reid (2023) suggests, and to ensure your emotions are respected and acknowledged in your relationships.

Think of physical boundaries as the invisible lines that mark your personal space. They relate to the physical contact you are comfortable with in different relationships. For example, you might feel comfortable with close physical contact with a family member but prefer a larger personal space with acquaintances. Physical boundaries help protect your comfort and safety, ensuring you are not pushed beyond your limits.

Psychological boundaries are all about your thoughts, goals, and dreams. Reid (2023) highlights that these boundaries can be as important as physical ones. It's essential to have your aspirations and values, even if they don't always align with those of your friends or partner. In a healthy relationship, both parties respect and support each other's psychological boundaries, even when their goals and dreams differ.

Boundaries aren't set in stone; they can evolve as circumstances shift and relationships grow. In long-term relationships, reevaluating and revising your boundaries may become necessary. As Reid (2023) emphasizes, communication is vital during this process. You want the other person to understand the changes and their reasons, ensuring that both parties are on the same page.

Sometimes, the boundaries you set for yourself are equally important. Self-betrayal can occur when you disregard your boundaries due to obligation, guilt, lack of awareness, or pressure (Das, 2023). It's essential to be mindful of your boundaries and not cross them to please others, as this can lead to self-betrayal.

Understanding and setting these boundaries in your relationships is vital for maintaining your well-being, personal safety, and individuality. Boundaries serve as the rules of engagement that ensure you can have healthy, fulfilling connections with those around you.

### The Importance of Boundaries

Boundaries are like the invisible lines that shape how you engage with others. Just as a fence around a garden keeps unwanted animals out, emotional and physical boundaries are your way of protecting your well-being in relationships. They are not meant to be exclusive or isolating; instead, they promote healthy interactions.

Healthy boundaries help to maintain a sense of respect and equality in relationships. When you have clear boundaries, it's easier to understand what you want from your connections, communicate your needs, and ensure that the relationships are mutually beneficial. Boundaries allow you to define your values, desires, and what you are willing to tolerate.

Setting boundaries may seem challenging at first, but it's a skill that can be learned and honed over time.

Start by reflecting on your values and emotional needs. Recognize situations where you have felt uncomfortable or stressed because your boundaries were not respected. Identifying these moments will help you pinpoint your limits.

Once you are aware of your boundaries, you must convey them effectively. You will learn to express your limits clearly and assertively without feeling rude or aggressive. Healthy communication can prevent misunderstandings and conflicts.

As you define your boundaries, remember that it's a reciprocal process. Others have their limits, too. Understanding and respecting their boundaries is key to fostering trust and maintaining harmonious relationships.

### Signs of Boundary Violations

Recognizing signs of boundary violations is essential to address issues early on. These signs may include feeling uncomfortable, stressed, or anxious in certain interactions. When you notice these signs, it's an opportunity to assess if your boundaries have been crossed and communicate your needs with the other person.

You create a framework for healthy, respectful, and fulfilling interactions by understanding, establishing, and respecting boundaries in your relationships. This approach allows you to protect your emotional well-being and ensure that your relationships are supportive, balanced, and rewarding.

## ACTIVITY: MAPPING YOUR EMOTIONAL GEOGRAPHY

Creating a relationship map is a powerful tool for understanding your emotional landscape and identifying areas where you can improve the health of your connections.

This activity will guide you through the process step by step:

**Step 1:** Identify your relationships

Start by making a list of your current relationships. This includes family, friends, romantic partners, acquaintances, and anyone you interact with regularly. You can use a notebook, a digital document, or a piece of paper.

**Step 2:** Define each relationship

Next to each relationship, describe the person's role in your life, the nature of the connection, and how you feel when you are with them. Be honest about your feelings, whether positive or negative.

**Step 3:** Assess the health of your relationships

For each relationship, consider the following factors to assess its health:

- **Trust:** Do you trust this person, and do they trust you in return?
- **Communication:** How well do you communicate with this person? Is it open and honest, or is there a lack of transparency?
- **Respect:** Do you feel respected in this relationship? Are your boundaries respected, and do you respect theirs?
- **Support:** Does this person support your emotional well-being? Are they there for you when you need them, and are you there for them?

- **Conflict:** How do conflicts get resolved in this relationship? Are they resolved healthily, or do they lead to more problems?

**Step 4:** Color-code your map

Using colored pens or markers, color-code your relationships based on their health.

For example:

- Green for healthy relationships
- Yellow for relationships with some issues
- Red for unhealthy or toxic relationships

**Step 5:** Reflect and set goals

Take a step back and look at your relationship map. What patterns do you notice? Are there specific areas where you see room for improvement? Reflect on why you categorized each relationship the way you did.

**Step 6:** Action plan

For relationships in the "yellow" or "red" categories, brainstorm actions you can take to improve their health. These actions might include better communication, setting boundaries, or seeking support from others. Create a plan to work on these areas over time.

**Step 7:** Maintain your relationship map

Regularly revisit your relationship map to assess your progress and track changes in the health of your connections. This map serves as a valuable tool for ongoing self-assessment and personal growth.

By mapping out your emotional geography, you gain clarity about your relationships and empower yourself to make choices that nurture your well-being. Remember, relationships are dynamic and can change, so regularly revisiting your map ensures you continue growing and maintaining healthy, fulfilling connections.

### *Affirmations: Speak Life Into Your Relationships*

Remember, these affirmations can be a source of inspiration and guidance when navigating your relationships. Whether you are going through a difficult time with a friend, family member, or partner, recite these affirmations to ground yourself, improve your self-worth, and build healthier connections. Affirmations are a wonderful tool for speaking life into your relationships and ensuring they remain nurturing and fulfilling.

### Self-Worth Affirmations

- "I am deserving of love, respect, and kindness."
- "I embrace my uniqueness and honor my true self."
- "I am enough just as I am, and I don't need to change for anyone."

**Setting Boundaries**

- "I am confident in my boundaries and communicate them."
- "I respect others' boundaries to show love and consideration."
- "I release the need to overcommit, and I prioritize self-care."

**Conflict Resolution**

- "I am open to healthy communication and approach conflicts with an open heart."
- "I am willing to forgive and let go of past hurts to create space for healing."
- "I value peaceful resolutions and approach conflicts with empathy and understanding."

**Empathy and Understanding**

- "I strive to see the world through others' eyes and understand their perspectives."
- "I practice empathy and actively listen to the feelings and concerns of those I care about."
- "I embrace compassion and aim to make others feel seen and heard."

## Building Trust

- "I am trustworthy and reliable in my relationships."
- "I give trust to receive trust, and I believe in the good intentions of others."
- "I choose to let go of past betrayals and open my heart to trust again."

## Gratitude for Relationships

- "I am grateful for the people who enrich my life with their presence."
- "I express my appreciation for the love and support I receive from my loved ones."
- "I cherish the connections that bring joy, growth, and meaning to my life."

## Self-Improvement

- "I am committed to personal growth and improving my communication skills."
- "I seek to understand my triggers and work on self-awareness to enhance my relationships."
- "I choose love over fear and strive to be the best version of myself in all my relationships."

# 8

# WHAT'S NEXT—YOUR ROADMAP TO AN AMAZING FUTURE!

In the enchanting world of Harry Potter, Hermione Granger is hailed for her intelligence, resilience, and resourcefulness. We've all been inspired by her character, yearning to embody her sense of empowerment. In the spirit of Hermione's wisdom, as J.K. Rowling so beautifully reminds us, we don't need a wand or a spellbook to transform our world; we already possess all the magic we need inside us. The power to shape our future brilliantly lies within our grasp.

Visualize yourself as the architect of your life, painting the canvas of your future with vibrant strokes of ambition, determination, and creativity. You are about to craft a vision board, a tangible representation of your dreams and aspirations. This powerful tool will assist you in manifesting your goals, keeping your aspirations alive, and providing clarity as you pursue a brighter tomorrow.

## LOOK HOW FAR YOU'VE COME!

As we venture through this final chapter of our transformative odyssey, it's essential to pause and reflect on your remarkable progress. Your path has been adorned with valuable insights, self-discovery, and remarkable personal growth.

Think back to the beginning of this journey, where you may have assessed your self-worth based on external factors, like the number of likes on a social media post. Yet, as you explored the importance of self-love, you learned to practice self-affirmations, celebrate your uniqueness, and prioritize intrinsic values. An example of your growth is your newfound ability to acknowledge that a day without social media validation doesn't diminish your worth. You have learned to feel genuinely content and confident, even when not conforming to unrealistic beauty standards.

You have delved into effective study techniques and time management. Perhaps you began the journey grappling with procrastination, but along the way, you harnessed the power of the Pomodoro Technique to enhance your focus and exam scores. Your growth is evident in your transition from struggling to plan study schedules to diligently organizing your study time, with your academic achievements reflecting your unwavering dedication.

You should now be equipped with strategies for understanding and managing your emotions. You might have started with little awareness of your emotional triggers, but gradually, you developed the ability to defuse them. Your growth shines through in your newfound knowledge to refrain from impulsive reactions when stress strikes. Now, you employ deep breathing exercises and grounding techniques to maintain composure and thoughtfulness, even in challenging situations.

You explored what makes relationships healthy and the vital role of boundaries. You may have realized you were tolerating toxic friendships or draining romantic relationships. But your growth is evident in your newfound ability to establish clear boundaries and the confidence to let go of relationships that do not uplift you. Perhaps you have surrounded yourself with friends who respect your boundaries and nurtured a more fulfilling romantic relationship.

As we look back at these instances of growth, it becomes clear how far you have come on this journey. The central message is that by applying the lessons and tools provided here, you possess the capacity to transform various facets of your life. Your growth in self-love, academics, emotional intelligence, and relationships demonstrates the incredible power of self-improvement and personal development.

Now, as you look forward to your future dreams and aspirations, know that this journey has equipped you to face the challenges and seize the opportunities. You have grown, evolved, and discovered the strength within you to make your dreams a reality. The path to your brilliant future is illuminated by the lessons learned, the wisdom gained, and the incredible potential within you. So, step forward confidently, for you are the author of your story, and the adventure continues!

Remember the wise words of Popomaronis (2019), "We do not need magic to change the world; we carry all the power we need inside ourselves already. We have the power to imagine better" (para. 15). Your journey has unfolded the magic within you. Now, you have the power to shape a brilliant future.

Throughout this journey, we have emphasized the significance of self-reflection. Self-reflection is like a mirror that allows you to look deeply within yourself and understand your thoughts, actions, and beliefs. As Amy Morin (2016) wisely notes, self-reflection involves deliberate thinking about your behavior and beliefs. It's an intentional act that enables you to develop an awareness of your mental and emotional states and an understanding of your actions. It forms the foundation for personal growth.

However, self-reflection can be like shining a light on the parts of yourself that you may not always want to see. As Perry (2022) aptly points out, it can sometimes be uncomfortable. It requires holding yourself accountable, admitting weaknesses, and actively striving for further personal development. At times, avoiding potentially harmful aspects of ourselves might seem more straightforward.

Yet, it's essential to remember that self-reflection is a powerful tool. Gupta (2023) highlights its significance, stating that self-reflection contributes to your self-concept, an integral part of your identity. Your self-concept includes thoughts about your traits, abilities, beliefs, values, roles, and relationships. It is crucial in your mood, judgment, and behavioral patterns.

Without self-reflection, as Gupta (2023) emphasizes, you might continue to follow the same patterns and routines, facing the same problems repeatedly. In contrast, self-reflection allows you to grow, evolve, and change your life for the better.

So, as you wrap up this journey, remember to continue the practice of self-reflection. It's your guiding light, helping you uncover your true self, identify areas for improvement, and continue on the path of self-discovery and personal growth.

## #GOALS ARE MORE THAN JUST A HASHTAG

Imagine your dreams as the North Star guiding you through the adventure of growing up. These dreams are more than wishes; they are your secret map to self-discovery and becoming the amazing person you are meant to be.

Goals act as the guiding lights on the journey of your dreams, much like planning the perfect road trip with your besties. They are like the North Star, bringing clarity to questions like, "What do I want to achieve?" and "Where do I want to be?" Think of them as the ultimate GPS for navigating through life's twists and turns, ensuring each step you take is purposeful and exciting.

When you set specific goals, it's like casting friendly spells that keep you committed and determined. Your desire to reach these goals becomes a secret potion, giving you the energy to keep moving forward, even when things get challenging.

As you track your progress, goals turn every achievement into a magical victory. They are milestones, showing you how far you've come and how close you are to turning your dreams into reality. Celebrating these small victories is like collecting magical treasures that boost your confidence and self-belief, making you feel unstoppable.

In essence, goals are the enchanting tools that transform your ordinary days into an extraordinary adventure. Embrace them as the magical keys to unlocking your dreams, creating a life story that's uniquely yours, filled with excitement and achievements. You're the hero of your own magical journey, and goals are there to guide you every step of the way!

Pursuing goals often leads to personal growth. It's like discovering new magical abilities within you. You step out of your comfort zone, gaining new skills, making memories, and finding hidden talents you never knew you had.

Achieving your goals is like unlocking a treasure chest of happiness and fulfillment. It proves that your magical spells and hard work have paid off. It's a beautiful reminder that your dreams are not just dreams but real adventures waiting to be experienced.

In a world full of possibilities and enchanting dreams, setting and working toward your goals is your magical wand, casting spells of empowerment and self-discovery. Your dreams are the spells, and you are the powerful magician. So, embark on your magic journey, for pursuing your dreams is an incredible adventure that's uniquely yours.

The psychology behind goal-setting is rooted in self-determination and intrinsic motivation. Understanding why goals work can inspire you to set and pursue them effectively:

- **Intrinsic motivation:** Goals that resonate with your values and desires are more motivating. Setting goals that matter to you makes you more likely to stay committed, even when challenges arise.
- **Habit formation:** Consistent actions toward your goals can lead to habit formation. When a desired behavior becomes a habit, it requires less conscious effort, and you are more likely to maintain it.
- **Feedback loop:** Setting goals creates a feedback loop. You set a goal, take action, receive feedback on your progress, and adjust your efforts accordingly. This feedback loop is a fundamental part of the learning and improvement process.
- **Influence of values:** Goals that align with your core values are more compelling. When you understand what truly matters to you, your goals become about achievement and living following your principles.

Setting and pursuing goals is a dynamic process involving external achievements and internal growth. As you embark on your journey of self-discovery and personal development, remember that your goals are your companions, guiding you toward a more fulfilling and purposeful life.

*Don't Just Wish: How to Actually Make Stuff Happen*

By integrating SMART goals into your life, you are equipping yourself with a practical blueprint for turning your dreams into reality. The SMART framework is your trusty guide, whether it's excelling academically, achieving personal growth, nurturing enriching relationships, or embracing a healthier lifestyle. It transforms your dreams into actionable steps, making them more achievable and tangible. So, don't just wish for your dreams to come true; make them happen with SMART goals as your companion, turning your dreams into attainable realities. Your aspirations and SMART goals guide your journey to success.

**Specific**

The more precise your goal, the easier it is to follow your path to success. Instead of saying, "I want to do better in school," let's get specific. For example, "I aim to boost my math grade from a C to a B this semester." Specific goals outline precisely what you want to achieve, leaving no room for ambiguity.

**Measurable**

Measurable goals help you keep tabs on your progress. Let's take the example of getting more exercise. To make it measurable, set a goal like, "I'll go for a 30-minute walk three times a week." This way, you can track whether you are meeting your target, and it's like a progress bar filling up.

## Achievable

Setting achievable goals means making them realistic. If you are keen on becoming a better public speaker, start with an achievable goal like, "I'll speak confidently in front of my class during the next presentation." It's more realistic than aiming for a TED Talk next month, allowing you to build your skills step by step.

## Relevant

Relevance is all about ensuring your goals align with your passions and dreams. If you are passionate about writing, a relevant goal might be, "I'll complete a 10,000-word novel by the end of the year." This goal ties into your interests and brings you closer to your writing dreams.

## Time-Bound

Setting a deadline keeps you on track. Instead of a vague goal like, "I'll learn to play the guitar someday," set a time-bound goal like, "I'll be able to play a simple song on the guitar within three months." Having a specific timeframe motivates you to work consistently.

### *Activity: Crafting Your Future Through a Vision Board*

Creating a vision board is an exciting and creative way to bring your dreams and aspirations to life. It's not just an artistic project; it's a powerful tool that can keep you focused on your goals and motivated to achieve them.

**Steps to Create Your Vision Board**

Before you begin, take a few moments to think about your goals and aspirations. What do you want to achieve? What areas of your life would you like to improve? This will guide your vision board creation.

Go through magazines, newspapers, or printouts, and cut out images and quotes representing your goals. These can relate to your academics, personal growth, relationships, or any other aspect of your life that's important to you.

Start arranging the images and quotes on your board. There's no right or wrong way to do this—let your creativity flow. You can group similar goals or create a collage that's visually appealing to you.

Once you are satisfied with your arrangement, attach everything to the board. Take your time to make sure it's well-organized.

You can use markers, colored pencils, stickers, or drawings to add a personal touch to your vision board. Write down your thoughts or affirmations related to your goals.

Find a special place for your vision board where you will see it regularly. This could be in your room, near your desk, or anywhere that works for you.

So, get creative and enjoy the process of crafting your vision board. It's not just a craft project; it's a tool to help you shape your future and make your dreams a reality. Remember, your vision board reflects your dreams and aspirations, so have fun, be authentic, and let your creativity guide you toward the future you desire.

### Final Affirmations and Takeaways

Congratulations on making it through this incredible journey of self-discovery and empowerment. As you step boldly into your future, remember that the power to shape your life is within you.

## Empowering Affirmations

- "I am enough, just as I am."
- "I trust in my abilities and my journey."
- "I am the author of my own story. I hold the pen."
- "My dreams are within reach, and I have the strength to achieve them."
- "I am resilient, and I can overcome any challenge."
- "I deserve love, respect, and happiness in all my relationships."
- "I am constantly growing and evolving into my best self."
- "I can shape my future and make my dreams a reality."

## Journal Prompts for Reflection

- What are my most significant goals and aspirations in life?
- How have I grown throughout this journey of self-discovery?

- What steps will I take to maintain and nurture the self-love I've developed?
- What positive changes have I noticed in my academic and personal life?
- How do I envision my future, and what practical steps will I take to achieve it?
- What have I learned about building healthy relationships, and how will I apply these lessons moving forward?

# CONCLUSION

We have reached the end of our adventure together, and what a ride it's been! You have journeyed through the pages of this book, discovering the tools and skills you need to unlock your true potential.

So, here's the key takeaway: You are a force of nature, capable of shaping your life in remarkable ways. Throughout this book, you've explored the art of self-love, honed your academic prowess, mastered emotional intelligence, and learned the secrets of building strong relationships.

As we close this chapter, take inspiration from the success stories you have encountered. Let their achievements fuel your dreams and aspirations.

Now it's your time to shine. Armed with newfound knowledge and a whole lot of girl power, venture forth with confidence.

You are ready to take on the world. Crush doubts and be the shining star you were always meant to be.

Thank you for being part of this empowering adventure. Your story is just beginning, and it's bursting with potential. Embrace it, live it, and show the world the incredible person you are!

# REFERENCES

Ackerman, C. (2018a, July 12). *What is self-acceptance? 25 Exercises + definition and quotes.* PositivePsychology.com. https://positivepsychology.com/self-acceptance/

Ackerman, C. (2018b, November 6). *What is self-Worth and how do we increase it?* PositivePsychology.com. https://positivepsychology.com/self-worth/

Adeeyo, O. (2023, July 27). *35 Daily affirmations for whatever you're going through.* Wondermind. https://www.wondermind.com/article/daily-affirmations/

Albano, A. M. (2021, May 20). *Is social media threatening teens' mental health and well-being?* Columbia University Irving Medical Center; Columbia University. https://www.cuimc.columbia.edu/news/social-media-threat ening-teens-mental-health-and-well-being

Alves, R. (2017, July 25). *What factors influence your self-esteem?* Essence of Healing Counseling. https://www.essenceofhealingcounseling.com/what-factors-influence-your-self-esteem/

American Psychological Association. (2018, November 1). *Stress effects on the body.* American Psychological Association. https://www.apa.org/topics/stress/body

Anchor Therapy. (n.d.). *How to help your teen to social media detox.* Anchor Therapy, LLC. https://www.anchortherapy.org/blog/how-to-help-your-teen-to-social-media-detox

Anderson, L. (2022, March 11). *Helping your teen detox from social media.* NewFolks. https://www.newfolks.com/stages/how-to-help-your-teen-to-detox-social-media/

Andrade, S. (2021, July 1). The importance of setting healthy boundaries. *Forbes.* https://www.forbes.com/sites/forbescoachescouncil/2021/07/01/the-importance-of-setting-healthy-boundaries/

Ankrom, S. (2021, March 20). *How to breathe properly for relieving your anxiety.* Verywell Mind. https://www.verywellmind.com/abdominal-breathing-2584115

Arcaya, A. (n.d.). *Subject guides: essential study skills: creating a weekly schedule.*

Algonquincollege.libguides.com. https://algonquincollege.libguides.com/studyskills/weeklySchedule

AspenRidge Recovery. (2021, January 23). *Types of peer pressure | negative peer pressure & addiction.* AspenRidge. https://www.aspenridgerecoverycenters.com/types-of-peer-pressure-5/

Banner Health. (2022, March 10). *How to tell the difference between good and bad stress | Banner.* Www.bannerhealth.com. https://www.bannerhealth.com/healthcareblog/teach-me/bad-stress-vs-good-stress-how-can-i-tell-the-difference

Barbayannis, G., Bandari, M., Zheng, X., Baquerizo, H., Pecor, K. W., & Ming, X. (2022). Academic stress and mental well-being in college students: Correlations, affected groups, and COVID-19. *Frontiers in Psychology, 13*(886344). https://doi.org/10.3389/fpsyg.2022.886344

Barker, E. (2016, April 26). *10 ways to boost your emotional resilience, backed by research.* Time. https://time.com/4306492/boost-emotional-resilience/

Bendory, S. (2023, March 1). *Signs you lack self-love (and how to develop it).* Thought Catalog. https://thoughtcatalog.com/sabrina-bendory/2023/03/signs-you-lack-self-love-and-how-to-develop-it/

Best Day . (2021, July 9). *Personal growth through self-reflection.* Best Day Psychiatry & Counseling. https://bestdaypsych.com/personal-growth-through-self-reflection/

BetterHealth. (2015, June 30). *Parent's guide for active children.* Www.better-health.vic.gov.au. https://www.betterhealth.vic.gov.au/health/HealthyLiving/parents-guide-for-active-girls

Bloemen, N., & De Coninck, D. (2020). Social media and fear of missing out in adolescents: The role of family characteristics. *Social Media + Society, 6*(4), 1–11. https://doi.org/10.1177/2056305120965517

Borenstein, J. (2020, February 12). *Self-Love and what it means.* Brain & Behavior Research Foundation. https://www.bbrfoundation.org/blog/self-love-and-what-it-means

Bouchrika, I. (2021, April 1). *Digital notes vs paper notes: Benefits of Taking Notes by Hand.* Research.com. https://research.com/education/digital-notes-vs-paper-notes

Box Communications. (2022, January 24). *The best note-taking methods.* Box Blog. https://blog.box.com/best-note-taking-methods

Broadbent, K. (2021). *Active vs. passive learning: what's the difference?*

Melioeducation.com. https://www.melioeducation.com/blog/active-vs-passive-learning/

Broadwater, A. (2022, July 8). *Toxic social accounts don't deserve your follow. Here are 8 ways to spot them.* HuffPost. https://www.huffpost.com/entry/toxic-social-media-account-signs_l_62c71ef5e4b02e0ac9118c35

Buffalmano, L. (2018, November 20). *7 signs of frenemies: How to spot a frenemy.* Power Dynamics™. https://thepowermoves.com/how-to-spot-a-frenemy/

Canada Mental Health Association. (2019, October 17). *The importance of human connection.* CMHA National. https://cmha.ca/news/the-importance-of-human-connection/

Capulet, S. (2019, February 3). *7 ways you may not realize your boundaries are being Crossed.* Thought Catalog. https://thoughtcatalog.com/sarah-capulet/2019/02/7-ways-you-may-not-realize-your-boundaries-are-being-crossed/

Carlton, G. (2022, May 13). *How to stop procrastinating in college: 7 tips | BestColleges.* Www.bestcolleges.com. https://www.bestcolleges.com/blog/how-to-stop-procrastinating/

Carroll, C. (2021, September 9). *20 body positive journal prompts for reflection and self-love.* Snacking in Sneakers. https://www.snackinginsneakers.com/body-positive-journal-prompts/

Carter, C. (2017, May 17). *How to handle a toxic relationship.* Greater Good. https://greatergood.berkeley.edu/article/item/how_to_handle_a_toxic_relationship

Castillo, L. (2023, April 5). *The most surprising self love statistics and trends in 2023 • GITNUX.* Gitnux. https://blog.gitnux.com/self-love-statistics/

Cattel, J. (2021, July 8). *10 ways to get your teen (and family) to try a digital detox.* Connecticut Children's. https://www.connecticutchildrens.org/mental-health/10-ways-to-get-your-teen-and-family-to-try-a-digital-detox/

Centerstone. (2022). *What is peer pressure and who is at risk?* Centerstone. https://centerstone.org/our-resources/health-wellness/what-is-peer-pressure-and-who-is-at-risk/

Cherry, K. (2021a). *The 6 types of basic emotions and their effect on human behavior.* Verywell Mind. https://www.verywellmind.com/an-overview-of-the-types-of-emotions-4163976

Cherry, K. (2021b, June 22). *Common signs of low self-esteem.* Verywell Mind. https://www.verywellmind.com/signs-of-low-self-esteem-5185978

Cherry, K. (2022, February 25). *Emotions and types of emotional responses.* Verywell Mind. https://www.verywellmind.com/what-are-emotions-2795178

Child Trends. (2015, June 24). *How teens benefit from healthy relationships with family and friends.* Child Trends. https://www.childtrends.org/blog/how-teens-benefit-from-healthy-relationships-with-family-and-friends

Chung, M. (2022, April 4). *Good vs. bad stress: How to tell the difference.* Talkspace. https://www.talkspace.com/blog/good-stress-vs-bad-stress/

Cooks-Campbell, A. (2022a, May 26). *What self-love truly means and ways to cultivate it.* Www.betterup.com. https://www.betterup.com/blog/self-love

Cooks-Campbell, A. (2022b, July 15). *Triggers: Learn to recognize and deal with them.* BetterUp. https://www.betterup.com/blog/triggers

Coursera. (2022, September 15). *11 good study habits to develop.* Coursera. https://www.coursera.org/articles/study-habits

Cowen, A. (2018). How many different kinds of emotion are there? *Frontiers for Young Minds, 6.* https://doi.org/10.3389/frym.2018.00015

Creative Resilience Counseling. (2019). *Journal prompts for teens and young adults.* https://kindnessmatters365.org/wp-content/uploads/2020/10/Journal-Prompts.pdf

Cromwelle, J. (2022). *25 scientifically proven tips for effective studying [2020 Edition].* MyDegreeGuide.com. https://www.mydegreeguide.com/how-to-study-tips/

Cronkleton, E. (2019, April 9). *10 breathing techniques.* Healthline; Healthline Media. https://www.healthline.com/health/breathing-exercise

Cuncic, A. (2018). *What does it mean to be "triggered?"* Verywell Mind. https://www.verywellmind.com/what-does-it-mean-to-be-triggered-4175432

Curran, T. (2022, March 31). *Rising parental expectations linked to perfectionism in college students.* Apa.org. https://www.apa.org/news/press/releases/2022/03/parental-expectations-perfectionism

Cut, the. (2020, May 12). *How to spot frenemies: 9 ways to tell you have a frenemy.* The Cut. https://www.thecut.com/article/how-to-spot-frenemies.html

Das, T. (2023, June 17). *Signs you are crossing your own boundaries.* Hindustan Times. https://www.hindustantimes.com/lifestyle/relationships/signs-you-are-crossing-your-own-boundaries-101687006658620.html

DeMeyer, B. (2021, August 26). *10 ways to evaluate the health of your relationship.* Mysite. https://www.sereneharbor.org/post/10-ways-to-evaluate-the-health-of-your-relationship

Donnelly, M. (2017, February 24). *5 ways You Can Filter Negativity From Your Social Media Feeds*. Thought Catalog. https://thoughtcatalog.com/marisa-donnelly/2017/02/5-ways-you-can-filter-negativity-from-your-social-media-feeds/

Dornelly, A. G. (2014, July 7). *8 key signs that you are lacking in self-love*. Www.lifecoach-Directory.org.uk. https://www.lifecoach-directory.org.uk/memberarticles/8-key-signs-that-you-are-lacking-in-self-love

Earley, B. (2021, March 24). *Stuck in a Rut? Consider Making a Vision Board*. Oprah Daily. https://www.oprahdaily.com/life/a29959841/how-to-make-a-vision-board/

Edubirdie. (2022, December 15). *Beauty Defined by Society - Free Essay Example*. Edubirdie. https://edubirdie.com/examples/beauty-defined-by-society/

Effectiviology. (2019). *Handwriting vs. typing: how to choose the best method to take notes* Effectiviology.com. https://effectiviology.com/handwriting-vs-typing-how-to-take-notes/

*11 facts about teens and self esteem*. (2015) DoSomething.org. https://www.dosomething.org/us/facts/11-facts-about-teens-and-self-esteem

Elizabeth, D. (2021, October 31). *54 Positive self-love affirmations to build your self-worth FAST! – Wild Simple Joy*. Wildsimplejoy.com. https://wildsimplejoy.com/affirmations-self-worth/

espeal. (2021, June 11). *90 Self-esteem resources for girls*. CORP-MAC0 (OCP). https://onlinecounselingprograms.com/resources/self-esteem-resources-girls/

Evans, T. (2021, September 23). *Using photo filters on social media: watch for the red flags*. https://www.nationwidechildrens.org/family-resources-education/700childrens/2021/09/social-media-photo-filters-red-flags

Fairfax County Public schools. (2019). *How to Handle Peer Pressure | Fairfax County Public Schools*. Fcps.edu. https://www.fcps.edu/student-wellness-tips/peer-pressure

Felton, A. (2022, November 9). *What are the different types of emotions?* WebMD. https://www.webmd.com/balance/what-are-the-different-types-of-emotions

Flower Aura. (2021, April 21). *The 5 most important elements Of a healthy relationship*. Floweraura Blog. https://www.floweraura.com/blog/5-most-important-elements-healthy-relationship

Fowler, P. (2018, January 11). *Breathing techniques for stress relief*. WebMD. https://www.webmd.com/balance/stress-management/stress-relief-breathing-techniques

Fox, J., & Vendemia, M. A. (2016). Selective Self-Presentation and Social Comparison Through Photographs on Social Networking Sites. *Cyberpsychology, Behavior, and Social Networking, 19*(10), 593–600. https://doi.org/10.1089/cyber.2016.0248

Fox, M. (2022, August 5). *13 Vision board benefits you can't ignore.* SelfMadeLadies. https://selfmadeladies.com/vision-board-benefits/

Franchina, V., Vanden Abeele, M., van Rooij, A., Lo Coco, G., & De Marez, L. (2018). Fear of Missing Out as a Predictor of Problematic Social Media Use and Phubbing Behavior among Flemish Adolescents. *International Journal of Environmental Research and Public Health, 15*(10), 2319. https://doi.org/10.3390/ijerph15102319

Garey, J. (2016, January 29). *How to help teenagers get more sleep.* Child Mind Institute; Child Mind Institute. https://childmind.org/article/help-teenagers-get-sleep/

Garrett, M. (2023, March 28). *Affirmations for teenage girls to use daily* Divas with a Purpose. https://www.divaswithapurpose.com/affirmations-for-teenage-girls/

Gavin, M. (2014). *Fitness and your 13- to 18-year-old (for Parents).* Kidshealth.org. https://kidshealth.org/en/parents/fitness-13-18.html

GIETU. (2022, May 4). *Why is emotional literacy essential?* GIET University. https://www.giet.edu/post/why-is-emotional-literacy-essential/

Godwin, K. (2023, January 24). The impact of social media on self-worth and how to use it. *Counselling Directory.* https://www.counselling-directory.org.uk/memberarticles/the-impact-of-social-media-on-self-worth-and-how-to-use-it

Gongala, S. (2015, July 22). *29 Impressive workout for teenage girls.* MomJunction. https://www.momjunction.com/articles/workout-plans-for-your-teenage-girl_00364027/

Gonzalez, A. (2023, January 6). *Healthy vs. unhealthy relationships.* WebMD. https://www.webmd.com/sex-relationships/healthy-vs-unhealthy-relationships

GoodTherapy. (2015, October 15). *Inner critic.* GoodTherapy.org Therapy Blog. https://www.goodtherapy.org/blog/psychpedia/inner-critic

Gordon, S. (2019). *Do you suffer from FOMO? Find out how to cope.* Verywell Family. https://www.verywellfamily.com/how-fomo-impacts-teens-and-young-adults-4174625

Gulotta, J. (2022, April 12). *Self-criticism: what it is, examples, & how to overcome.* Choosing Therapy. https://www.choosingtherapy.com/self-criticism/

Gupta, S. (2023, May 26). *How self-reflection can improve your mental health.* Verywell Mind. https://www.verywellmind.com/self-reflection-impor tance-benefits-and-strategies-7500858

Hanson, J. (2022, May 10). *The social media complex: confusing self-love with narcissism.* DGN Omega. https://dgnomega.org/13286/opinion/the- social-media-complex-confusing-self-love-with-narcissism/

Hartney, E. (2022, October 6). *What is peer pressure?* Verywell Mind. https:// www.verywellmind.com/what-is-peer-pressure-22246

healthychildren.org. (2019). *For teens: creating your personal stress-management plan.* HealthyChildren.org. https://www.healthychildren.org/English/ healthy-living/emotional-wellness/Building-Resilience/Pages/For-Teens- Creating-Your-Personal-Stress-Management-Plan.aspx

Hinde, N. (2017, December 15). *10 Women share powerful stories of self-love.* HuffPost UK. https://www.huffingtonpost.co.uk/entry/in-your-skin- women-share-their-journey-of-self- acceptance_uk_5a33b29de4b01d429cc7cdf6

Holz, A. (2022, April 19). *How social media distorts reality.* Plugged In. https:// www.pluggedin.com/blog/how-social-media-distorts-reality/

Hong, S., Jahng, M. R., Lee, N., & Wise, K. R. (2020). Do you filter who you are?: Excessive self-presentation, social cues, and user evaluations of Instagram selfies. *Computers in Human Behavior, 104,* 106159. https://doi. org/10.1016/j.chb.2019.106159

Hovey, L. (2019, July 31). *How social media can distort reality.* Conscious Counselling. https://www.consciouscounselling.co/post/how-social- media-can-distort-reality

Hsieh, C. (2023, July 24). *4 Ways to social-media proof your brain—from TikTok therapists who get it.* Wondermind. https://www.wondermind.com/article/ social-media-mental-health/

Hutchinson, T. (2018, May 21). *Why are personal boundaries important? Your rights in a relationship.* Tracy Hutchinson, PhD | Fort Myers Therapy. https://www.drtracyhutchinson.com/what-are-personal-boundaries-and- why-are-they-important/

Hutchison, M., & Campbell, A. (2020, September 15). *12 elements of healthy relationships.* Johns Hopkins University Student Well-Being. https://wellbe ing.jhu.edu/blog/2020/09/15/12-elements-of-healthy-relationships/

Jacobson, R. (2022, September 2). *Social media and self-doubt*. Child Mind Institute. https://childmind.org/article/social-media-and-self-doubt/

Jhangiani, R., & Tarry, H. (2014, September 26). *The social self: the role of the social situation – principles of social psychology – 1st international edition*. Opentextbc.ca. https://opentextbc.ca/socialpsychology/chapter/the-social-self-the-role-of-the-social-situation/

Jines, R. (2017, September 19). *Beauty standards of society could lead to misconceptions with self image*. Texan Mosaic. https://texanmosaic.com/2017/09/19/beauty-standards-of-society-could-lead-to-misconceptions-with-self-image/

John Muir Health. (2019). *Nutrition for teens*. Johnmuirhealth.com. https://www.johnmuirhealth.com/health-education/health-wellness/childrens-health/nutrition-teens.html

Kassir, Y. (2021, March 16). *Unrealistic body standards create toxic environment*. The Standard. https://standard.asl.org/17556/opinions/unrealistic-body-standards-create-toxic-environment/

Keithley, Z. (2021a, July 26). *33 Journal prompts for goal setting & future planning*. Zanna Keithley. https://zannakeithley.com/journal-prompts-for-goal-setting/

Keithley, Z. (2021b, October 4). *45 Goal affirmations for achieving your dreams*. Zanna Keithley. https://zannakeithley.com/goal-affirmations/

Kelly, A. (2019, January 16). *Take charge of your health: A guide for teenagers*. National Institute of Diabetes and Digestive and Kidney Diseases. https://www.niddk.nih.gov/health-information/weight-management/take-charge-health-guide-teenagers

Kids Helpline. (2017, September 11). *What to do when you're feeling the peer pressure*. Kids Helpline. https://kidshelpline.com.au/teens/issues/peer-pressure-and-fitting

Klammer, S. (2021, May 1). *The purpose of your inner critic*. Depth Therapy. https://www.shelleyklammer.com/post/the-purpose-of-your-inner-critic

Klier, C., & Buratto, L. G. (2020). Stress and long-term memory retrieval: a systematic review. *Trends in Psychiatry and Psychotherapy*, *42*(3), 284–291. https://doi.org/10.1590/2237-6089-2019-0077

Kristenson, S. (2021, December 6). *70 Affirmations for self worth and love yourself more*. Happier Human. https://www.happierhuman.com/affirmations-self-worth/

Kristenson, S. (2022, January 31). *50 Affirmations for getting good grades in school*. Happier Human. https://www.happierhuman.com/affirmations-good-grades/

Kristenson, S. (2023, March 20). *Toxic vs healthy relationship: 7 important differences*. Happier Human. https://www.happierhuman.com/toxic-vs-healthy-relationship-wa1/

Lamia, M. C. (2012). *Emotions!* American Psychological Association.

Langlois , C. (2015, March 23). *Great self-esteem exercise for teens: the mirror exercise*. Dr Carol. https://dr-carol.com/2015/03/23/great-self-esteem-exercise-for-teens-the-mirror-exercise/

Laplante, S. (2022, January 9). *How social media can crush your self-esteem*. The Conversation. https://theconversation.com/how-social-media-can-crush-your-self-esteem-174009

Laundry, M. (2019, June 18). *The super easy self esteem activity - the mirror exercise*. Miriam Laundry. https://miriamlaundry.com/the-mirror-exercise-self-esteem-activity-for-children-and-adults/

Lawler, M. (2021, December 30). *How to do a digital detox*. EverydayHealth.com. https://www.everydayhealth.com/emotional-health/how-to-do-a-digital-detox-without-unplugging-completely/

Leinwand, L. (2017, January 31). *What does it mean to feel beautiful?* Www.goodtherapy.org. https://www.goodtherapy.org/blog/what-does-it-mean-to-feel-beautiful-0131175

Lily-Jo Project. (2022, August 17). *Top 18 self-care resources of 2022 for teens and adults*. The Lily Jo Project. https://www.thelilyjoproject.com/2022/08/17/top-18-self-care-resources-of-2022-for-teens-and-adults/

Llopis, G. (n.d.). *7 Ways to value yourself beyond social media*. Forbes. Retrieved October 28, 2023, from https://www.forbes.com/sites/glennllopis/2013/03/11/7-ways-to-value-yourself-beyond-social-media/

Loic, L. (2023, March 21). *6 Ways to curate your social media feeds to improve your mental wellness*. MUO. https://www.makeuseof.com/curate-social-media-feeds-improve-mental-wellness/

Lorenz, T. (2021, March 19). *5 Myths of the self-love movement*. Taylor's Tracks. https://www.taylorstracks.com/5-myths-of-the-self-love-movement/

Lyness, D. (2019). *5 Ways to prevent stress buildup (for teens) - KidsHealth*. Kidshealth.org. https://kidshealth.org/en/teens/stress-tips.html

Madariola, O. (2017, October 20). *The general misconception about physical beauty*. Www.linkedin.com. https://www.linkedin.com/pulse/general-misconception-physical-beauty-zoe-oluwabusayo-madariola/

Magsambol, B. (2017, April 14). *6 ways to get rid of negativity on social media.* RAPPLER. https://www.rappler.com/technology/social-media/166788-get-rid-negativity-social-media/

Marks, H. (2021). *Stress symptoms.* WebMD. https://www.webmd.com/balance/stress-management/stress-symptoms-effects_of-stress-on-the-body

Martin, S. (2019, May 31). *What is self-love and why is it so important?* Psych Central. https://psychcentral.com/blog/imperfect/2019/05/what-is-self-love-and-why-is-it-so-important

Mayo Clinic . (2022, February 26). *Teens and social media use: what's the impact?* Mayo Clinic; Mayo Foundation for Medical Education and Research. https://www.mayoclinic.org/healthy-lifestyle/tween-and-teen-health/in-depth/teens-and-social-media-use/art-20474437

Mayo Clinic Staff. (2021, March 24). *Stress management.* Mayo Clinic; Mayo Clinic. https://www.mayoclinic.org/healthy-lifestyle/stress-management/in-depth/stress-symptoms/art-20050987

Mayo Clinic Staff. (2022, January 12). *Friendships: enrich your life and improve your health.* Mayo Clinic. https://www.mayoclinic.org/healthy-lifestyle/adult-health/in-depth/friendships/art-20044860

Mind Tools Content Team. (2022). *Personal goal setting.* Www.mindtools.com. https://www.mindtools.com/a5ykiuq/personal-goal-setting

MindWise Innovations. (2017, July 24). *The importance of social connection.* MindWise. https://www.mindwise.org/blog/uncategorized/the-importance-of-social-connection/

Morin, A. (2021, July 29). *10 Ways to help your teen deal with a breakup.* Verywell Family. https://www.verywellfamily.com/how-to-help-your-teen-deal-with-a-breakup-4047445

Morin, A. (2022, September 1). *Negative and positive peer pressure differences.* Verywell Family; Verywellfamily. https://www.verywellfamily.com/negative-and-positive-peer-pressure-differences-2606643

Morin, S. (2016, December 13). *Five tips on self-reflection for personal growth | HealthyPlace.* Www.healthyplace.com. https://www.healthyplace.com/blogs/livingablissfullife/2016/12/self-reflection-a-valuable-tool-for-personal-growth

Muffett, I. (2021, April 7). *Understanding peer pressure, misconceptions.* Common Sense. https://woottoncommonsense.com/9852/features/understanding-peer-pressure-misconceptions/

National Center for Chronic Disease Prevention and Health Promotion. (2023, May 8). *How Does Social Connectedness Affect Health?* Centers for Disease Control and Prevention. https://www.cdc.gov/emotional-wellbeing/social-connectedness/affect-health.htm

Nariman, J. (2021, January 4). *How to help teens set effective goals (tips & templates).* Big Life Journal. https://biglifejournal.com/blogs/blog/guide-effective-goal-setting-teens-template-worksheet

Nationwide Children's. (2021). *Sleep in adolescents.* Nationwidechildrens.org. https://www.nationwidechildrens.org/specialties/sleep-disorder-center/sleep-in-adolescents

Nationwide's Children. (n.d.). *Healthy sleep habits for older children and teens.* Www.nationwidechildrens.org. https://www.nationwidechildrens.org/family-resources-education/health-wellness-and-safety-resources/helping-hands/healthy-sleep-habits-for-older-children-and-teens

Nemours Teen Health. (2018). *Easy exercises for teens.* Kidshealth.org. https://kidshealth.org/en/teens/easy-exercises.html

NHS. (2021, February 3). *Tips on preparing for exams.* Nhs.uk. https://www.nhs.uk/mental-health/children-and-young-adults/help-for-teenagers-young-adults-and-students/tips-on-preparing-for-exams/

Office of Population Affairs. (2022). *Healthy relationships in adolescence.* Opa.hhs.gov. https://opa.hhs.gov/adolescent-health/healthy-relationships-adolescence

Office on Women's Health. (2019, April 30). *Helping your teen through an unhealthy relationship.* Womenshealth.gov. https://www.womenshealth.gov/blog/unhealthy-teen-relationships

Opt Health. (2020, October 20). *Why a holistic approach to health is important.* Opt Health. https://getopt.com/2020/10/20/holistic-approach-health/

Ozimek, P., Lainas, S., Bierhoff, H.-W., & Rohmann, E. (2023). How photo editing in social media shapes self-perceived attractiveness and self-esteem via self-objectification and physical appearance comparisons. *BMC Psychology, 11*(1). https://doi.org/10.1186/s40359-023-01143-0

parentingteensandtweens. (2022, April 5). *More than 30 positive affirmations For Your Teen To Help Their Confidence and Mental Health.* Parentingteensandtweens.com. https://parentingteensandtweens.com/more-than-30-positive-affirmations-for-your-teen-to-help-their-confidence-and-mental-health/

Paul, M. (2015, April 17). *What emotional triggers are + why you need to under-*

*stand them*. Mindbodygreen. https://www.mindbodygreen.com/articles/emotional-triggers

Peer, A. (2022, January 14). *Active learning vs. passive learning*. Learn to Win. https://www.learntowin.com/blog/active-passive-learning-differences

Perkins, K. (2017, January 11). *How society defines beauty*. Frontline. https://elmodenafrontline.com/11929/showcase/how-society-defines-beauty/

Perry, E. (2021, August 5). *The path to self-acceptance*. BetterUp. https://www.betterup.com/blog/self-acceptance

Perry, E. (2022a, April 13). *Healthy boundaries in relationships: a guide for building and keeping*. Www.betterup.com. https://www.betterup.com/blog/healthy-boundaries-in-relationships

Perry, E. (2022b, December 21). *Self-reflection: learn how to better understand yourself*. Www.betterup.com. https://www.betterup.com/blog/self-reflection

Perry, E. (2023, June 15). *5 Steps to create a vision board that does its job*. Www.betterup.com. https://www.betterup.com/blog/how-to-create-vision-board

Pontz, E. (2018, September 4). *Peer pressure: strategies to help teens handle it effectively*. Center for Parent and Teen Communication. https://parentandteen.com/handle-peer-pressure/

Popomaronis, T. (2019, March 28). *J.K. Rowling's greatest advice to Harvard grads is disturbingly dark—but honestly, so brilliant and true*. CNBC. https://www.cnbc.com/2019/03/28/harry-potter-novelist-jk-rowling-famous-advice-to-harvard-students-is-dark-but-so-brilliant-and-true.html

Port St Lucie Hospital. (2021, May 7). *Identifying emotional triggers: common triggers & what they mean*. Port St. Lucie Hospital, Inc. | Florida Mental Health Services. https://www.portstluciehospitalinc.com/identifying-emotional-triggers-common-triggers-what-they-mean/

Perspectives. (n.d.). *Holistic therapy for self esteem - boost your self-confidence!*. Perspectives Center for Holistic Therapy. Retrieved October 26, 2023, from https://www.perspectivesholistictherapy.com/self-esteem-therapy

Preston, E. (2018, March 6). *3 Tips for more effective note taking methods*. Connections Academy. https://www.connectionsacademy.com/support/resources/article/3-tips-effective-note-taking-methods/

Raaziya, S. (2023, February 20). Dominating beauty standards: 4 reasons why high beauty standards are dangerous. *The Times of India*. https://time

sofindia.indiatimes.com/readersblog/awesome-reads/dominating-beauty-standards-4-reasons-why-high-beauty-standards-are-dangerous-50709/

Rahman, I. (2022, August 26). *How to leave a toxic relationship*. Choosing Therapy. https://www.choosingtherapy.com/how-to-leave-a-toxic-relationship/

Raypole, C. (2020, November 13). Emotional triggers: Definition and how to manage them. *Healthline*. https://www.healthline.com/health/mental-health/emotional-triggers

ReachOut Parents. (2020). *Stress management for teens*. Reachout.com. https://parents.au.reachout.com/common-concerns/everyday-issues/things-to-try-stress/manage-stress-with-relaxation

Reed, J. A. (2022, March 5). *How social media distorts the truth about everything we know*. New York Post. https://nypost.com/2022/03/05/how-social-media-distorts-the-truth-about-everything-we-know/

Reid, S. (2023, March 1). *Setting healthy boundaries in relationships*. Https://Www.helpguide.org/. https://www.helpguide.org/articles/relationships-communication/setting-healthy-boundaries-in-relationships.htm

Republica. (2020, January 14). *"Myth Busters": Beauty lies in the eyes of beholder*. My City. https://myrepublica.nagariknetwork.com/mycity/news/myth-busters-beauty-lies-in-the-eyes-of-beholder

Reynolds, N. (2022, August 18). *75 Positive self-esteem boosting affirmations for teens*. Raising Teens Today. https://raisingteenstoday.com/75-positive-self-esteem-boosting-affirmations-for-teens/

Reynolds, P. (2022, November 10). *Managing stress in high school*. Harvard Summer School; Harvard Division of Continuing Education. https://summer.harvard.edu/blog/managing-stress-in-high-school/

Ridgeview Behavioral Hospital. (2021, May 15). *How to identify emotional triggers in 3 steps*. Ridgeview Behavioral Hospital. https://ridgeviewhospital.net/how-to-identify-emotional-triggers-in-3-steps/

Riopel, L. (2019, June 14). *The importance, benefits, and value of goal setting*. PositivePsychology.com. https://positivepsychology.com/benefits-goal-setting/

Robledo, I. (2022, January 15). *Self esteem journal prompts for teens*. Making Mindfulness Fun. https://www.makingmindfulnessfun.com/self-esteem-journal-prompts-teens/

Rood, E. (2021, March 30). *Self-esteem affirmations for teens | teen coach advice*.

Inspire Balance. https://www.inspirebalance.com/10-self-esteem-affirma tions-for-teens/

Roosevelt, E. (n.d.) *Eleanor Roosevelt quotes.* BrainyQuote. https://brainyquote. com/quotes/eleanor_roosevelt_161321

Rosenberg, L. (2022, April 8). *The problem with social media is not content but its distortion of reality.* Big Think. https://bigthink.com/the-present/social-media-distorts-reality/

Roy Chowdhury, M. (2019, January 22). *What is emotional resilience? (+6 proven ways to build it).* PositivePsychology.com. https://positivepsychology.com/emotional-resilience/#google_vignette

Royster, M., & Hogan, S. (2021, January 8). *How to filter your social media feeds.* NBC4 Washington. https://www.nbcwashington.com/news/consumer/how-to-filter-your-social-media-feeds/2533133/

Russell, K. (2021, June 2). *Active vs. passive learning: what's the difference?* Graduate Programs for Educators. https://www.graduateprogram.org/2021/06/active-vs-passive-learning-whats-the-difference/

Russell, L. (2022, November 19). *SMART goals for teens: help your teen to happiness and success.* They Are the Future. https://www.theyarethefuture.co.uk/smart-goals-teens/

Ryan, T. (2021, May 13). *Why sleep can help you ace your final exams.* Sleep Foundation. https://www.sleepfoundation.org/school-and-sleep/final-exams-and-sleep

Sandi, C. (2018). *Memory impairments associated with stress and aging.* Nih.gov; CRC Press/Taylor & Francis. https://www.ncbi.nlm.nih.gov/books/NBK3914/

Schaffner, A. K. (2020, October 15). *Living with your inner critic: 8 helpful worksheets and activities.* PositivePsychology.com. https://positivepsychology.com/inner-critic-worksheets/

Scott, E. (2007, June 15). *Top 10 school stress relievers for students.* Verywell Mind; Verywellmind. https://www.verywellmind.com/top-school-stress-relievers-for-students-3145179

Scott, E. (2018, February 12). *How stress works with and against your memory.* Verywell Mind; Verywellmind. https://www.verywellmind.com/stress-and-your-memory-4158323

Scott, E. (2020, April 28). *8 Traits that can make you more emotionally resilient.* Verywell Mind. https://www.verywellmind.com/emotional-resilience-is-a-trait-you-can-develop-3145235

Scott, S. (2020, June 24). *67 Positive affirmations for teens to boost self-confidence.* Happier Human. https://www.happierhuman.com/positive-affirmations-teens/

Seppala, E. (2014, May 9). *Connectedness & health: the science of social connection - The Center for Compassion and Altruism Research and Education.* The Center for Compassion and Altruism Research and Education. https://ccare.stanford.edu/uncategorized/connectedness-health-the-science-of-social-connection-infographic/

Seppälä, E. (2020, March 23). *Social connection boosts health, even when you're isolated | Psychology Today.* Www.psychologytoday.com. https://www.psychologytoday.com/us/blog/feeling-it/202003/social-connection-boosts-health-even-when-youre-isolated#:

Serai, P. (2023, January 1). *Frenemies: who they are, types & 29 signs and ways to see & handle them.* LovePanky - Your Guide to Better Love and Relationships. https://www.lovepanky.com/my-life/relationships/understand-frenemies

7Mindsets. (2016, June 7). *Goal setting for teens.* 7 Mindsets. https://7mindsets.com/smart-goal-setting-for-students/

Shafer, L. (2017, December 15). *Social media and teen anxiety | Harvard Graduate School of Education.* Www.gse.harvard.edu. https://www.gse.harvard.edu/ideas/usable-knowledge/17/12/social-media-and-teen-anxiety

Share Your Happiness. (n.d.). *The importance of social connection and why you need it In your life.* Shape Your Happiness. Retrieved October 26, 2023, from https://www.shapeyourhappiness.com/the-importance-of-social-connection-and-why-you-need-it-in-your-life/

Sharma, S. (2022, September 3). *7 Free resources for teenagers to help regain self-confidence & self-esteem.* Calm Sage - Your Guide to Mental and Emotional Well-Being. https://www.calmsage.com/resources-for-teenagers-to-regain-self-confidence/

Shatz, I. (2023). *Student procrastination: why students procrastinate and how to stop it – solving Procrastination.* Solving Procrastination. https://solvingprocrastination.com/student-procrastination/

Sheldon, C. M., & Tudor, A. (2022, August 7). *50 Self-esteem boosting affirmations for teens.* Mindvalley Blog. https://blog.mindvalley.com/affirmations-for-teens/

Silva Casabianca, S. (2022, October 28). *Signs your boundaries are being violated:*

*examples and how to deal.* Psych Central. https://psychcentral.com/relation
ships/signs-boundary-violations

Smith, S. (2023, April 28). *10 Key elements of a healthy relationship.* Marriage
Advice - Expert Marriage Tips & Advice. https://www.marriage.com/
advice/relationship/elements-of-a-healthy-relationship/

Stabler, C. (2022). *Brain power: 10 tips for creating good study habits.* Lancaster-
generalhealth.org.    https://www.lancastergeneralhealth.org/health-hub-
home/2021/august/brain-power-10-tips-for-creating-good-study-habits

Staff Writers. (2019, March 13). *Stress management in school: tips for parents,
teachers, & students.* AccreditedSchoolsOnline.org; AccreditedSchoolsOn-
line.org.    https://www.accreditedschoolsonline.org/resources/student-
stress/

Steckler, S. (n.d.). *The biggest myths about self-love debunked.* Sarah Steckler |
Plan & Publish. Retrieved October 17, 2023, from https://sarahsteckler.
com/blog/the-biggest-myths-of-self-love-debunked

Stoker, J. (2020, September 14). *How to assess the quality of your relationships.*
Www.dialogueworks.com.    https://www.dialogueworks.com/blog/how-
to-assess-the-quality-of-your-relationships

Straw, E. (2023a, September 8). *Importance of goal setting.* Www.suc-
cessstartswithin.com.    https://www.successstartswithin.com/blog/impor
tance-of-goal-setting

Straw, E. (2023b, September 8). *The secret to building new habits.* Www.suc-
cessstartswithin.com.    https://www.successstartswithin.com/blog/why-
self-discipline-habits-go-hand-in-hand

Suni, E., & Dimitriu, A. (2023, October 4). *Sleep for teenagers.* Sleep
Foundation; Sleep Foundation. https://www.sleepfoundation.org/teens-
and-sleep

Taibbi, R. (2017, August 13). *10 Questions to assess the state of your relationship |
Psychology Today.* Www.psychologytoday.com. https://www.psychologyto
day.com/us/blog/fixing-families/201708/10-questions-assess-the-state-
your-relationship

Talk It Out. (2019, November 26). *What are the 6 types of peer pressure?* Talk It
Out. https://www.talkitoutnc.org/types-of-peer-pressure/

Tamm, S. (2021, May 25). *The 7 best study methods for all types of students.* E-
Student. https://e-student.org/best-study-methods/

Team, Q. (2023, March 14). *Online peer pressure: what to know and how to support kids.* Qustodio. https://www.qustodio.com/en/blog/curbing-the-effects-of-digital-peer-pressure/

The Jed Foundation. (n.d.). *Student stress 101: understanding academic stress | JED.* The Jed Foundation. https://jedfoundation.org/resource/understanding-academic-stress/

The Life Blog. (2021, October 4). *100 Positive affirmations for students.* Gratitude - the Life Blog. https://blog.gratefulness.me/positive-affirmations-for-students/

Thomas, S. (2016, October 7). *A virtual life - how social media changes our perceptions.* Insight Digital Magazine; The Chicago School of Professional Psychology. https://www.thechicagoschool.edu/insight/from-the-magazine/a-virtual-life/

Travers, M. (2023, April 12). *Psychologists define what the term "frenemy" really means.* Forbes. https://www.forbes.com/sites/traversmark/2023/04/12/psychologists-define-what-the-term-frenemy-really-means/

Trettenero, S. (2017, April 13). *Human beings are first and foremost emotional creatures.* Psychreg. https://www.psychreg.org/human-beings-are-first-foremost-emotional-creatures/

Tritsch, E. (2022, January 1). *How to set goals for teens - the SMART goals method.* Fairborn Digital Academy. https://fairborndigital.us/2022/01/01/smart-goals-for-teens/

Trout, S. (2019, July 11). *6 Tips to create the perfect study environment.* Herzing University. https://www.herzing.edu/blog/6-tips-create-perfect-study-environment

University of Alabama Division of Student Life Counseling Center. (n.d.). *Healthy vs. unhealthy relationships.* Counseling Center. https://counseling.sa.ua.edu/resources/healthy-vs-unhealthy-relationships/

University of St. Augustine. (2020, January 30). *10 Effective study techniques to try this year.* University of St. Augustine for Health Sciences. https://www.usa.edu/blog/study-techniques/

University of Tennessee at Chattanooga. (2021). *Common note-taking methods | University of Tennessee at Chattanooga.* Www.utc.edu. https://www.utc.edu/enrollment-management-and-student-affairs/center-for-academic-support-and-advisement/tips-for-academic-success/note-taking

University of Utah. (2023, January 20). *The impact of social media on teens' mental health.* University of Utah Health | University of Utah Health.

https://healthcare.utah.edu/healthfeed/2023/01/impact-of-social-media-teens-mental-health

UNSW Sydney Current Students . (n.d.). *Techniques and tips for listening and note taking*. Www.student.unsw.edu.au. https://www.student.unsw.edu.au/notetaking-tips

Voge, D. (2007). *Understanding and overcoming procrastination*. McGraw Center for Teaching and Learning; Princeton University. https://mcgraw.princeton.edu/undergraduates/resources/resource-library/understanding-and-overcoming-procrastination

Wake Forest University. (2020, June 26). *School stress management for students of all ages | Wake Forest University*. WFU Online Counseling. https://counseling.online.wfu.edu/blog/school-stress-management-for-students/

Warwick Wellbeing and Student Support. (2022, March 16). *Emotional resilience*. Warwick.ac.uk. https://warwick.ac.uk/services/wss/topics/emotional_resilience/

Weiss, J. (2022, December 1). *How FOMO impacts teens - FamilyEducation*. Www.familyeducation.com. https://www.familyeducation.com/teens/health/mental/how-fomo-impacts-teens

Whyte, A. (2021, July 20). *Social media and anxiety in youth: how social media can lead to anxiety in teens*. Evolve Treatment Centers. https://evolvetreatment.com/blog/social-media-anxiety-teens/

wikiHow. (2009a, September 14). *Create a study schedule*. wikiHow. https://www.wikihow.com/Create-a-Study-Schedule

wikiHow. (2009b, October 26). *Prepare for an exam*. wikiHow. https://www.wikihow.com/Prepare-for-an-Exam

wikiHow, Ruiz, A., & Tieperman, J. (n.d.). *14 Ways to relax before a final exam in college*. WikiHow. Retrieved October 29, 2023, from https://www.wikihow.com/Relax-Before-a-Final-Exam-in-College

Williamson, J. (2020, March 10). *13 Affirmations for feeling your feelings*. Healing Brave. https://healingbrave.com/blogs/all/affirmations-feeling-your-feelings

Woda, S. (2014). *7 Obvious signs your teen is suffering from peer pressure*. Uknowkids.com. https://resources.uknowkids.com/blog/7-obvious-signs-your-teen-is-suffering-from-peer-pressure

Wong, S. J. (n.d.). *13 Things that don't determine your self-worth*. Shine. https://advice.theshineapp.com/articles/12-things-that-dont-determine-your-self-worth/

Wooll, M. (2022a, February 7). *Self-criticism and how to overcome it.* Www.betterup.com. https://www.betterup.com/blog/self-criticism

Wooll, M. (2022b, February 24). *A quick guide to develop discipline – how to be disciplined.* Www.betterup.com. https://www.betterup.com/blog/how-to-be-disciplined

Wright, A. (2020, October 25). *15 Signs that your boundaries need work.* Annie Wright, LMFT. https://www.anniewright.com/15-signs-that-your-boundaries-need-work/

Young, K. (2016, March 23). *Toxic relationships: how to let go when it's unhappily ever after.* Hey Sigmund. https://www.heysigmund.com/toxic-relationship-how-to-let-go/

Your Therapy Source. (2022, August 11). *SMART goals for teens.* Your Therapy Source. https://www.yourtherapysource.com/blog1/2022/08/11/smart-goals-for-teens-3/

youth.gov. (n.d.). *Characteristics of healthy & unhealthy relationships.* Youth.gov. Retrieved October 25, 2023, from https://youth.gov/youth-topics/teen-dating-violence/characteristics